ALLISS' 19TH HOLE

Trivial Delights from the World of Golf

ALLISS'
19TH HOLE

Trivial Delights from the World of Golf

Peter Alliss with Rab MacWilliam

Da Capo Press
A Member of the Perseus Books Group

Illustrations by BrindeauMexter

Cataloging-in-Publication data for this book is available from the Library of Congress.

First Da Capo Press edition 2006
Originally published in Great Britain in 2005 by Arcane, an imprint of Sanctuary Publishing; reprinted by arrangement.

ISBN-13: 978-0-306-81488-4 (hardcover)
ISBN-10: 0-306-81488-9 (hardcover)

Published by Da Capo Press
A Member of the Perseus Books Group
http://www.dacapopress.com

Da Capo Press books are available at special discounts for bulk purchases in the U.S. by corporations, institutions, and other organizations. For more information, please contact the Special Markets Department at the Perseus Books Group, 11 Cambridge Center, Cambridge, MA 02142, or call (800) 255-1514 or (617) 252-5298, or e-mail special.markets@perseusbooks.com.

1 2 3 4 5 6 7 8 9—09 08 07 06

— FOREWORD —

Nobody really knows when the game of golf began. Of course, for generations the Scots have claimed it as their own, but there have also been many rumblings from the Dutch, who are very quick to say, 'No, no, hold on a minute. We were playing a form of golf long before the Scots.' I'm sure that, if you look very closely, you'll find some Stone Age drawings depicting what appear to be people knocking round objects about with sticks!

The game of golf is a huge subject, and there's no doubt that it's been played in one form or another for at least 500 years. The glory of the game is that it's not a shared-ball game, so there's no physical aggression; plenty of mental stress but not too many bloody noses. In the words of David Forgan, it's a science, a contest, a duel, calling for courage, skill, self-control and strategy. It's always a great test of temper and a trial of honour, a revealer of character.

Henry Longhurst, with whom I worked for so many years on BBC Television, always used to say how fortunate we were that golf took us to so many beautiful places. Of course, there are grand football stadiums and cricket grounds, but even the most modest golf courses usually have shrubs, trees, flora and fauna, and a tranquillity not given to many games. The game of golf provides the opportunity for social intercourse, as well as an environment where the very best player can, because of the handicapping system, have a good match against a very modest player.

Golf is a mirror of life: everything is there to be seen, and a person's game, on many occasions, is a reflection of their own personality. You can call a man anything but a cheat in golf. If you do, that stigma stays forever.

Golf is a game replete with sadness and joy, courage, inexplicable happenings and, above all, great humour. I hope you enjoy this collection of stories and trivia. They cover a whole variety of happenings, a great many of them true (although, I have to confess, one or two may be apocryphal). And who knows? When you come to the end of these pages, if you're not a golfer now, you might just be tempted onto those green acres to have a go. Enjoy!

P. Alliss

Peter Alliss
June 2005

— INTRODUCTION —

Of all the world's major sports, the glorious game of golf is undeniably the one that most sharply divides popular opinion. While millions bask in the memories of the accidental overhead goal in the under-nines kickabout in the playground, indulge the delusion of the perfect swing of the bat that sent the ball gliding to a home run in the Cincinnati Little League or fondly remember the 400m relay at the school sports day, golf is generally absent from their ageing recollections. Why? Because, for most people (Scots apart), golf was simply not a youthful option, and the sport – for such it most certainly is – has long been regarded as an elitist activity, its frivolous pleasures restricted to a handful of wealthy plutocrats with too much time and money on their hands.

Golf, the argument continues, is a game for middle-aged, middle-class white men who stroll around a seemingly inexhaustible stretch of expensive real estate, pulling (rarely carrying) expensive technology designed to hit a white ball into a tiny hole a very long way away while attempting to surpass each other in the vulgarity of their clothing, opinions and abilities in this most apparently pointless of activities. What does this have to do with sport?

Well, if you play the game, you understand, and if you don't, then generally you don't. While golf, in some Neanderthal enclaves, still does its worst to live up to these accusations, the mass appeal of this endlessly absorbing and unpredictable game has never been greater. For every reactionary, boorishly opinionated country-club bigot there are – and always have been – countless thousands of golfing enthusiasts who are obsessed by golf and its unique, tantalising and frustrating challenge. And, unlike the aforementioned childhood memories, golf is far from a team game. There can be few other sports in which, when confronted by a serious problem, you look around for help and quickly realise, with a growing sense of panic, that it's entirely up to you. No one else will help, and there's no one else to blame. The ball just sits there, unmoving, passively awaiting your instructions. The result of your contact is either a joyful re-affirmation of your supreme, God-given ability to master this most existentially difficult of sports or a barely suppressed urge to strangle your opponent, who you're convinced fiddled with his car keys on your downswing.

As this book demonstrates, although technical golfing ability varies profoundly between the prodigiously talented, albeit robotic millionaires who prowl the immaculate fairways of the USPGA Tour and the besotted but fairly useless rest of us, there is a God (or, perhaps, club secretary) of golf. He or She takes delight in manipulating the vagaries of the game, the often hilarious, undignified and ridiculous situations that lie in ambush as we trudge from hole to hole in the vain pursuit of golfing excellence, all the while sadly aware that, despite the odd accidental birdie, our nemesis inevitably awaits. The facts, anecdotes, incidents and observations included in the book demonstrate the varied and compelling nature of this exasperating yet most addictive of games, and underline the unfortunate truth that no golfer – from Tiger Woods to Bert up the road – can ever expect perfection. All we can do is play it as it lies and hope for the best.

Rab MacWilliam
London, June 2005

— THE QUOTABLE ALLISS —

'Looks like a couple of Shetland ponies have been mating in there.'
*– On Richard Zokor's attempts to extricate himself from
the Road Hole bunker at St Andrews*

'You can't trust anybody these days.'
*– After US Walker Cup golfer Doug Clarke blessed himself before
trying a bunker shot and left the ball in the sand*

'Here he comes, the Queen Mother of golf. All he needs is a couple of
corgis.'
*– As Gary Player walked onto Royal Lytham's last green
during the 2001 British Open*

'You really couldn't find two more completely different personalities than
these two men, Tom Watson and Brian Waites. One is the complete golf
professional, the other the complete professional golfer.'

'Gosh, what an enormous one for such a little chap!'
– On a drive by Jose Rivero

'Five five five four seven. It's like the dialling code for Tierra del Fuego.'
*– Describing Duffy Waldorf's first five holes in the
second round of the 2002 British Open Championship*

'Oh, I'm not sure this is the right move.'
*– On Jean Van de Velde taking out his driver on the 18th tee
in the final round of the 1999 British Open at Carnoustie*

'If he gets that ball out, I'm retiring.'
*– On Jean Van de Velde in the Barry Burn,
Carnoustie, 1999 British Open*

'In technical terms, he's making a real pig's ear of this hole.'

ALLISS: 'What do you think of the climax of this tournament?'
PETER THOMSON: 'I'm speechless.'
ALLISS: 'That says it all.'

'Oh dear, he's here again. Chloroform, nurse, please.'
– On hearing a spectator shout, 'Get in the hole!'

'It's coming up to four hours, which, by modern standards, is almost Linford Christie stuff.'

– On slow play during the 2002 Ryder Cup

'Looks a bit like Jurassic Park in there.'

– On the rough at the 14th hole at Royal St George's.

'That's ridiculous. That's totally ridiculous. That's completely impossible. He'll have to go and have a lie down now.'

– After Phil Mickelson holes a 100ft putt.

'I can remember, before you found all sorts around the Open, when the only thing you could buy was a doughnut from a tea-shop.'

— UNDER 60: GOLF'S FOUR-MINUTE MILE —

For virtually all golfers, shooting 59 on a regular course is a wild dream. The first man on record to shoot sub-60 was Sam Snead at the unofficial Greenbrier Classic in (when else?) 1959.

The first professional to record a 59 on the US Professional Tour was Al Geiberger on 10 June 1977, in the Danny Thomas Memphis Classic at the Colonial Country Club, although preferred lies were in operation and Geiberger could lift, clean and place the ball. His total included 11 birdies, one eagle and just 23 putts. The score was eventually equalled by Chip Beck in Las Vegas in 1991 and, more recently, by David Duval in the 1999 Bob Hope Classic, in which Duval shot a 28 on the back nine.

Annika Sorenstam became the first woman on the LPGA Tour to shoot 59, at the 2001 Standard Register Ping tournament, also taking 28 on the homeward nine. The lowest recorded total on a long course in the UK is 58, scored by British Ryder Cup golfer Harry Weetman on the 6,170-yard Croham Hurst Course in Croydon, Surrey, on 30 January 1956. In the USA, Shigeki Maruyama also scored 58 in a qualifying round of the US Open at the Woodmount Country Club in Washington, DC, four months after Duval's 59.

— THE TALE OF BABE ZAHARIAS —

Arguably the greatest female athlete of the 20th century, Mildred Ella Didrickson Zaharias was born in Texas in 1911 of Norwegian stock. A sports prodigy as a young girl, she was nicknamed 'Babe' after baseball star Babe Ruth for her ability to smash the baseball out of sight. She excelled at every sport she took up, including basketball, baseball, swimming, track and field and tennis. When asked once if there was any sport she didn't play, she replied, 'Yeah, dolls.' In the 1932 Los Angeles Olympics, she won gold in the hurdles and javelin and silver in the high jump, having already won many other track and field events in her younger years.

Zaharias was introduced to golf in 1933 by US sports writer Grantland Rice and was soon hitting 1,000 balls a day in practice, her hands normally blistered by the effort. She was barred from amateur events by the USGA because of her status as a professional athlete, and throughout the 1930s she toured the States, playing exhibition matches with such golfers as Gene Sarazen, who insisted that she was the finest woman golfer he had ever seen.

With a colourful, belligerent and egocentric personality, Babe wasn't always popular with her fellow female competitors, but she paid little attention to such matters, knowing that on the golf course she was virtually unbeatable. Although she was slim and of average height, she could hit the golf ball over 250 yards. When asked how she did it, she replied, 'You've got to loosen your girdle and let it rip.'

Babe's amateur status was restored in 1943 and three years later she won the 1946 US Women's Amateur Championship, beating Clara Sherman 11 and 9 in the 36-hole final. The following year she became the first American to win the British Ladies' Amateur

Championship, and between 1946 and 1947 she won 17 tournaments in a row.

Babe turned professional in 1949, was a founding member of the Ladies' Professional Golf Association and was also the first lady professional at a golf club. In 1948 and 1950 she won the US Women's Open, a title she won again in 1953, after recovering from an operation for cancer. By 1955 she had claimed 31 professional victories, but was told that year that her cancer had returned and was now terminal and inoperable. After a courageous struggle with the disease, she died, in terrible pain, in September 1956 at the age of 45.

A tomboy as a kid, Babe eschewed traditional 'female' behaviour in her attitude and dress, and, although she had married wrestler George Zaharias in 1939, her closest and most intimate friend was fellow golfer Betty Dodd, which in the eyes of many confirmed her lesbian sexuality. A social pioneer, Babe broke out of the stifling straitjacket of societal expectations and became a trailblazer for future generations of American women. Voted Woman Athlete of the Year on six occasions by Associated Press, her obituary in UK newspaper *The Guardian* was headlined, 'DEATH OF WORLD'S GREATEST ATHLETE'.

— EXTREME GREENS —

The world's longest golf course is the International Golf Club in Massachusetts, a long par 77 and 8,325 yards from the championship tees. The world's largest green is that of the same club's 695-yard fifth hole, a par six, with an area in excess of 28,000sqft.

The longest hole in the world is at the Satsuki Golf Club in Japan, where the Sano Course's seventh hole (par seven) measures a whopping 909 yards. Currently under construction at Chocolay Downs, Michigan, however, is a 1,007-yard par six.

— ALLISS' HALL OF FAME: ARNOLD PALMER —

If any one man turned golf from an elitist pastime to one played and watched by millions, that man was Arnold Palmer. The emergence of this son of a Philadelphian golf professional coincided with the birth of the TV age to create a new image for golf as a sport for the common people.

At his first Major trophy, the 1958 Masters, Palmer electrified the galleries with his dynamic, swashbuckling strokeplay and Devil-may-care attitude, and 'Arnie's Army' – his band of supporters – was born. Palmer's aggressive style – smashing the ball for seemingly miles, and then doing the same thing again – excited his loyal fans and made him the focus of every tournament in which he played. Palmer grabbed golf by the scruff of the neck and dragged it into the modern age, teaming up with agent Mark McCormack in a move that eventually brought millions into his pocket and into the sport generally.

In 1960 Palmer won the Masters again as well as the US Open, breathing new life into this hallowed but essentially backwater event and shooting 30 on the front nine of the last round to beat Nicklaus by two strokes. He won the PGA Money List in 1958, 1960, 1962 and 1964, and the List is now referred to as the Arnold Palmer Award. He won his first British Open title at Birkdale in 1961 and won again by six shots at Troon the following year.

Palmer made his 35th and final appearance in the competition at St Andrews in 1995. In his golden period up until the mid-1960s he won two more Masters (1962 and 1964) and was US Player of the Year in 1960 and 1962. He won his last US Tour tournament – the Bob Hope Classic – in 1973, giving him 61 Tour victories, the fourth highest ever behind Sam Snead, Jack Nicklaus and Ben Hogan. He also played in six Ryder Cup teams (1961, 1963, 1965, 1967, 1971 and 1973).

In 1980 Palmer joined the fledgling Seniors' Tour and won the PGA Seniors' Championship that year. He won ten Seniors' Tour events and has earned over $13 million on it. He owns Bay Hill Golf Club in Orlando, and the Bay Hill Invitational has become a regular event on the USPGA Tour.

— POET LAUREATE OF THE LINKS —

One of America's finest ever amateur golfers, Charles 'Chick' Evans nonetheless played in seven US Amateur Opens without winning any of them. Indeed, he wrote a verse about his inability to win:

> I've a semi-final hoodoo, I'm afraid.
> I can never do as you do, Jimmy Braid.
> I've a genius not to do it,
> I excel at almost to it,
> But I never can go through it, I'm afraid.

This all changed in 1916, however, when Evans – an ex-caddie who had developed a foolproof way to find a missing ball by rolling around in the rough until his body encountered a small, round object – struck gold. Armed only with seven wood-shafted clubs – jigger, mashie, spoon, brassie, lofter, niblick and putter – he entered that year's US Open, held at Minikahda Country Club, Minneapolis, opening with a 32 on the first nine and ending his first round with a 70. (Many players of the time often carried a set of 20 clubs or more.) He continued with a 69, 74 and 73 to win the tournament on a score of 286, which remained unbeaten for 20 years. Ten weeks later, he won the US Amateur Open at Merion Cricket Club, Philadelphia, 4 and 3 over Bob Gardner.

Evans is in good company, as he and Bobby Jones are the only American golfers ever to have won the US Open and Amateur titles in the same year. He is also the only golfer to have played in 50 consecutive US Amateur Opens, contesting his final tournament in 1962 at the age of 72.

— A SENSE OF CLOSURE —

Craig Stadler once hit a drive under a low-growing pine tree in the 1987 San Diego Open at Torrey Pines, California, and was able to hit his second shot only by kneeling on the ground. Laying a towel on the ground to protect his trousers from the pine resin, Stadler took his shot. The next day, TV viewers phoned in to complain that, under Rule 13.3, he had technically 'built a stance', which is illegal. As he had already filled in and handed over his card, and hadn't added a two-stroke penalty, he had submitted a score lower than his real score and was disqualified. Several years later, he was invited back to the golf course and was offered a chain saw and asked if he would like to cut down the tree. He accepted with alacrity.

— BALLS AND IRONS: THE ORIGIN OF THE SPECIES —

Although the first golf balls were wooden, by the 17th century the projectile of choice was the 'feathery' ball, which was made of feathers stuffed and sewn into leather casings. A reputable manufacturer, such as Robertson's of St Andrews, could manufacture three to four a day, at most, and they were correspondingly expensive. The disadvantage of the feathery – aside from the fact that it priced many people off the golf course – was that it had a tendency to burst if hit badly or too hard.

In 1848, the development of the gutta-percha ball changed the nature of the game. Made of rubber from the Malayan percha tree, such balls were solid and could be remoulded back into shape if damaged. ('It's nae gowff,' said Mr Robertson, as you might expect.) Given the durability of the 'guttie', it was no longer necessary to use narrow-faced, slender wooden clubs, and shorter, broader-faced clubs such as the 'brassie' (two-wood) , 'mashie' (five-iron) and 'niblick' (nine-iron) became the norm. 'Irons' were now overtaking the traditional wooden-faced clubs, the resilience of the guttie accommodating the greater force of the new metal-faced clubs, although the shafts continued to be made of bamboo, ash or hickory.

All this changed towards the end of the 19th century with the innovation of the 'Haskell ball', created by American inventor Coburn Haskell, who devised a structure in which lengths of rubber were wound around a solid core, introducing spring and length to the ball. Sandy Herd won the 1902 British Open using the Haskell ball. Goodbye guttie.

As for the size of a golf ball, in 1921 the R&A (Royal and Ancient Golf Club of St Andrews – see Glossary) decided on a diameter of 1.62in, while ten years later the USGA increased the size to 1.68in. Although the British size offered the average golfer more distance and control, the American ball had more 'feel' and was the choice of better golfers and professionals. In 1987 the American size was classed as mandatory by the R&A.

Alongside the changing technology of golf balls, in the early years of the 20th century the wooden shafts of golf clubs came to be replaced with steel ones, an irreversible shift that was legalised in Britain in 1929 by the R&A. Numbers soon replaced the old, familiar club names (come back, the 'spoon'), and in 1939, in a move to prevent players from seeking unfair advantage, the number of clubs in a bag was limited to 14 by the USGA, followed the next year by the R&A. This remains the limit today, although at the 2001 British Open someone forgot to inform Ian Woosnam's unfortunate caddie, who packed 15 clubs. His mistake cost Woosnam a two-shot penalty and the lead, prompting the Welshman to fume, 'I give you one job to do and you can't even get that right!'

Nowadays, although steel is the preferred material for clubs, graphite, titanium and boron are all making their mark. Interestingly, although today it's rare to see players using wooden-headed clubs, they are still referred to as 'woods'.

— THE LIFE AND TIMES OF JOHN PATRICK DALY —

John Daly is one of the most watchable and skilful players in world golf. His phenomenal length off the tee, propelled by a spine-threatening, dizzying backswing (his motto is 'grip it and rip it'), accompanied by his accurate long- and mid-iron play and his feathery, delicate touch around the green, have brought him to the pinnacle of the game.

Daly is far from the average, whiter-than-white pro, however, and not for nothing is he known as 'Wild Thing'. His much-publicised problems with alcohol, women, his own temper and the USPGA have dogged him throughout his career, but his popularity and rapport with the US golfing public have helped him to overcome his failings, and he is his own man. How many other Tour members drive between tournaments in a 90ft recreational vehicle, complete with three 42in plasma TVs? Have any other top golfers recorded a country-music CD (tracks include 'All My Ex's Wear Rolexes' and 'I'm Drunk [And Broke]') documenting their rollercoaster careers? And who else in the Tour would dare to sport a mullet quite as extravagant as our man? (It's now, thankfully, gone.)

Here's a brief guide to some of the milestones in John's life to date, along with some episodes best forgotten:

1966   Born in Carmichael, California. Starts playing golf at the age of four and has his first beer at eight.

1987   Leaves the University of Arkansas and turns pro.

1991   Nick Price pulls out of the USPGA Championship to be at the birth of his child on the eve of the tournament. The first eight alternates cannot make the tournament, so the ninth and last, John Daly, packs his beer and drives through the night to Crooked Stick in Indiana, a course he has never played before. The podgy, long-haired unknown shoots 69, without a practice round, on the first round and then, to the astonishment of the seasoned pros and TV commentators, adds 67–69–71. Daly becomes an immediate favourite with the crowds and high-fives his way around the final round, beating Bruce Lietzke by three strokes to become USPGA champion. He ends his astonishing first season 17th on the Money List and is voted Rookie of the Year.

Later in the year he trashes a South Africa hotel room while drunk.

1992 Wins his second PGA Tour event, the BC Open, by six strokes, but is also put off a plane at Denver for drunkenly arguing with a stewardess. In December Daly is charged with third-degree assault of his then-wife Bettye, although the case is subsequently dropped. John enters rehab for the first time.

1993 Picks up his ball at the Kapula International in November after three successive double bogeys and is banned by the USPGA for three months.

1994 Earns his third Tour victory – helped by a second-round 64 – in the BellSouth Classic, holding off the challenges of Nolan Henke and Brian Henninger. In August Daly has a tussle with a 61-year-old man after shooting 81 at the World Series of Golf.

1995 Wins his second Major, claiming the British Open at St Andrews. At the end of the third round Daly has shot 67–71–73, including one shot where he reaches the green of the 316-yard 12th with a one-iron and the 567-yard 14th with a driver and a six-iron, to score 71 on his final round. Costantino Rocca is the only man who can catch him, and the Italian needs a birdie on the 18th to force a playoff. Rocca fluffs his second shot from the Valley of Sin but sinks an incredible 70-foot birdie putt. Daly wins the four-hole strokeplay playoff by 15–19.

1997 Splits up with his second wife, Paulette, and undergoes six weeks of alcohol rehabilitation at the Betty Ford Clinic. Daly opens with a 66 at the USPGA but takes a 77 in the next round, then throws his clubs into the nearby woods. He is dropped by his sponsor, Wilson, and signs a deal with Callaway for $10 million – enough to pay off his gambling debts.

1998 Plays alongside Tiger Woods and Mark O'Meara in the Dunhill Cup, unbeaten in his four games. Daly

— THE LIFE AND TIMES OF JOHN PATRICK DALY —
(CONT'D)

also scores 18 on the par-five sixth hole at the Bay Hill Invitational, landing his ball in the water six times.

1999   Callaway cancel their contract, claiming that Daly has reneged on an agreement not to drink or gamble.

2000   Undergoing a personal and professional slump, Daly reaches the 18th hole of the first round of the US Open at Pebble Beach at three over par. When asked earlier what he thought the winning score might be, he replied, 'Not mine.' He was right. His tee shot goes out of bounds and his next two land in the ocean. Another shot ends up in the water and he then has to chip left-handed out of a bunker. He finishes with a 14 and withdraws, pleading, 'Get me to the airport, fast.' His world ranking collapses to 507th place.

2001   Things improve and Daly wins the BMW International Open, his first win on the European Tour since 1995. His season's earnings total just under $830,000 and he ends up 61st on the Money List. He marries his fourth wife, Sherrie.

2002   Not such a successful year, although he wins the Tour Driving Distance for the 11th time with a record average of 306.8 yards,

2003   A bad year for Daly, who drops outside the world Top 200 rankings and withdraws, is disqualified or misses the cut in 16 of the 22 US Tour tournaments he enters. Although he wins the Korean Open on the Asian Tour, he has only one top-ten finish on Tour, at the Shell Houston Open. On top of this, there's more rehab and Sherrie is indicted for laundering drug money just five days after their son, John Daly, Jr, is born. She later plea-bargains and is sentenced to five years' probation.

2004   Things must improve, and they do. Still free of

alcohol, but addicted to cigarettes and cola, Daly wins the Bay Hill Invitational, hitting a bunker shot from 100ft to within 4in of the pin to win the three-man playoff, his first US Tour triumph in 189 tournaments. He then comes fourth in the Nissan Open and then, later in the season, is second to Vijay Singh in the Buick Open, earning more than $1 million overall. He is disappointed not to be included as a wild card in the Ryder Cup but, as he says about team captain Hal Sutton, 'I'm not going to kiss anyone's ass.'

Despite his occasionally reprobate behaviour, Daly is a big-hearted and generous man who is involved with and supports many charities. David Davies in *The Guardian* wrote recently of seeing him on a practice round at the USPGA at Whistling Straits where, on catching up with the group ahead and hearing that one of their number was organising a charity event to pay his daughter's medical bills, he went back to his motorhome, scooped up an armful of caps, club covers, shirts and CDs – which he normally sells to fans – and donated them to the charity. He also emptied his pockets, giving the startled father over $1,000. It's not difficult to understand why the Wild Thing is so popular with golf fans.

— WRONG FOOT FORWARD —

At the 1953 Masters, Count de Benden – otherwise known as Johnny de Forest – found his ball stuck in the bank of the stream in front of the 13th green. He decided that his best option was to play the ball and so took off his left shoe and sock and rolled up his left trouser leg. He then carefully placed his bare foot on the bank and, to the consternation of the gallery, stepped into the water with his right foot.

— ENDURANCE GOLF 1 —

Floyd Satterlee Rood used the United States as a golf course when he played from the Pacific coast to the Atlantic between 14 September 1963 and 3 October 1964. In all, he played a total of 114,737 strokes and lost 3,511 balls on the 3,397.7-mile trail.

— ALLISS' HALL OF FAME: BEN HOGAN —

A loner and perfectionist from an underprivileged background, Texan Ben Hogan was 34 years old before he won his first Major, the 1946 USPGA, but in the following seven years he establish himself as a golfing legend.

For such a relatively small man, 'Bantam' Ben was surprisingly long off the tee, and with his supremely accurate and consistent long game, honed by unstinting practice, he dominated US golf in the late 1940s and early 1950s. Hogan began with victories in the US Open and USPGA in 1948, but his career was interrupted by a serious car accident in 1949, leaving him with internal injuries, a double pelvic fracture and broken collarbone, ankle and rib. His injuries forced him out of the game for over a year, and even after that he found walking painful. A dogged and determined individual with little time for doubt and self-pity, he fought his way back into golfing contention and won his second US Open title in 1950 at Merion, then won it again in 1951 after a final-round 67 at Oakland Hills ('If I had to play this course every week, I'd go into some other business,' he commented) before triumphing in the Masters the same year.

Hogan's finest year was 1953, when he picked up his fourth US Open title at Oakmont (beating Sam Snead by six strokes), won again in the Masters and was victorious in the British Open at Carnoustie, the only occasion he entered the tournament and, indeed, the only time he ever played in the British Isles. On his return from Carnoustie, he was given a ticker-tape parade in New York.

Hogan never again won a Major, although he came close on several occasions, coming second at the 1955 and 1960 US Open and in the 1954 and 1955 Masters. He won a total of 63 US Tour events, with only Sam Snead and Jack Nicklaus winning more. He also wrote the classic golf instruction book *The Modern Fundamentals Of Golf*, with Herbert Warren Wind, and the Hollywood biopic of his life, *Follow The Sun*, starring Glenn Ford, was made in 1951. Hogan died in 1997.

— CELEBRITY GOLF —

'Every rock 'n' roll band I know, guys with long hair and tattoos, plays golf now.'

– Alice Cooper

In recent years, golf has shaken off its dowdy image. Contemporary celebrities who play the game include Jack Nicholson and Alice Cooper (both off single-figure handicaps), Willie Nelson (who owns a golf course in Texas), Neil Young, Bob Dylan, Joe Pesci, Smokey Robinson, Meat Loaf, Madonna, Dennis Hopper, Lou Reed, Samuel L Jackson, Will Smith and Sly Stallone, among many others.

From a slightly earlier generation, in the UK 'comedians' Jimmy Tarbuck and Bruce Forsyth and chat-show host Michael Parkinson are known for their love of the game, while in the USA Bing Crosby, Bob Hope, Groucho Marx, Jack Lemmon, Howard Hughes and WC Fields were all devotees. Actor-comedian *Caddyshack* star Bill Murray still plays on pro-ams, notably at the Pebble Beach Pro-Am, where his antics are much appreciated by the gallery, and Clint Eastwood, mayor of neighbouring Carmel, is also a golfer. And talking of actors/politicians, Arnold Schwarzenegger, the mayor of California, enjoys the occasional game. Finally, one of the 20th century's icons of cool was a keen golfer, if the authenticity of pictures showing Che Guevara dressed in his combat fatigues and swinging a five-iron is to be believed.

— CUP HISTORY —

Why is the diameter of the cup 4.25in? The origins of this lie with Musselburgh links, just outside Edinburgh, where in 1829 the first-ever hole-cutting tool was used. In 1893, the R&A (Royal and Ancient Golf Club of St Andrews) ruled that golf holes all over the world should be the same size, deciding that the holes at Musselburgh should be the model used. Those holes happened to be 4.25in wide, so this diameter was adopted everywhere and has been used ever since, even when the larger 1.68in-diameter golf ball was adopted in the USA in 1931.

— THE RULE OF LAW... —

If you're a golfing obsessive, *Decisions On The Rules Of Golf* – issued by the USGA and the R&A – is your Kama Sutra. This small-format, tightly packed tidal wave of questions sent in by golfers on all aspects of the game is accompanied by the adjudications by the ruling bodies. Some are straightforward, some are abstruse and some are almost Jesuitic in their complexity and interpretation. A few – such as those listed below – make you wonder whether or not the people who submitted them have a proper perspective on life. (Interpretations are also included for those readers who really want to know.)

1. A mushroom is growing on a player's line of putt. Is the player entitled to relief?

2. A ball lands against a dead crab in a bunker. May the crab be removed without penalty?

3. A player's ball lies under a parked car. What is the procedure?

4. A player's ball is lodged high in a tree. He identifies it with the aid of his binoculars (*binoculars?*) but is unable to retrieve it. Is the ball lost, in which case the player must invoke Rule 21.7?

5. May a player open the door of a barn to enable him to play a shot through the barn?

6. Is a snake an outside agency or a loose impediment?

Interpretations (abbreviated):

1. The player should stop play and ask the Committee (*what, all of them?*) to remove the mushroom.

2. Complex, but no.

3. Depends on whether the car is or is not movable.

4. No. Here, Rule 28 applies.

5. Yes. The barn is an immovable obstruction but the doors are movable.

6. If it's live, it's an outside agency. If it's dead, it's a loose impediment. But if it's not moving, who's going to check out the difference?

— ...AND THE CODE OF CONDUCT —

In the *Decisions On The Rules of Golf*, etiquette comes first and foremost and is concerned with courtesy, safety and care of the course. The main points to remember are:

- When playing a shot or a practice swing, ensure that nobody is standing within range of the club.

- The player with the 'honour' (ie who has won the previous hole) tees off first.

- Accompanying players should remain silent and immobile when a player is preparing to strike the ball.

- Before taking a shot, the player should make sure that any players ahead are out of range.

- Players should play 'without delay'. If a ball is difficult to find, the players behind should be signalled to pass through. Players should immediately leave the putting green when each hole is completed. In professional golf, players can be fined shots if the referee judges that their pace of play is too slow.

- Two-ball matches have precedence over three- and four-ball matches and should be signalled through. A single player has no status and should give way to any other match. A match playing a whole round has precedence over a match playing a shorter round.

- Footprints and holes in bunkers should always be smoothed over after use. All divots should be replaced. All marks made by a ball on the green should be repaired. Damage to the green by the spikes of golf shoes should be repaired, but only after the hole is completed. The flagstick should be replaced in the hole when players have completed the hole. Players should not lean on their putters on the putting green.

Other golfing etiquette not specified in the Rules:

- If a ball is heading towards a player or group of players, shout 'Fore left' or 'Fore right' to warn them.

- On the green, do not walk across the line of other players' putts.

- Do not tee off if players are putting out on an adjacent green.

- Players should always offer to hold the flagstick if an accompanying player is ready to putt.

— THE GREAT BATTLES OF GOLF HISTORY 1 —

ARNOLD PALMER V JACK NICKLAUS, US OPEN, CHERRY HILLS, 1960

Fresh from his second Masters victory, 31-year-old Arnold Palmer was toiling before the final round of the US Open. He lay seven strokes behind Mike Souchak, five behind Ben Hogan and four behind a 20-year-old, blond-haired amateur named Jack Nicklaus. Before the final round, he speculated that, if he shot 65, he would win. When a sceptical journalist questioned this, Palmer replied, 'A 65 would give me 280, and 280 wins Opens.'

Palmer hit a 350-yard drive off the first tee and birdied the first hole, then followed this up by birdying the next three holes to reach the turn in 30. Meanwhile, Souchak's challenge was fading and Nicklaus could only play to par. Accompanied by his fanatical fans, 'Arnie's Army', Palmer slowed down somewhat over the back nine but finished his round on 65 – exactly as he had predicted – to win the tournament. Hogan blew his chance of a tenth Major championship by taking a six and a seven on the 17th and 18th, while Nicklaus ended two shots behind Arnie in second place. Hogan said of Nicklaus, 'I played 36 holes today with a kid who should have won this thing by ten strokes.' Nicklaus was soon to turn professional and his rivalry with Palmer was only just beginning.

— A LONG DRIVE —

The longest recorded drive ever recorded on an ordinary course was one of 515 yards by Michael Hoke Austin of Los Angeles, California, in the US National Seniors' Open Championship at Las Vegas, Nevada, on 25 September 1974. On that occasion, Austin drove the ball within a yard of the green on the par-four, 450-yard fifth hole of Winterwood Course, where it duly rolled 65 yards past the flag, aided by an estimated 35mph tailwind.

— A TYPICAL GOLF HOLE —

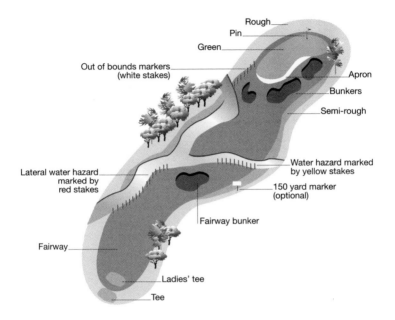

— ROBBERY —

Scott Hoch and his wife booked into a local motel before the 1982 Tucson Open. During the night, thieves broke into the room, tied up the Hochs and made away with $4,500. Despite this experience, Hoch finished 15th in the tournament…winning $4,500.

— ENDURANCE GOLF 2 —

The longest delayed result in any national open championship occurred at the Inverness Golf Club, Toledo, Ohio, in the 1931 US Open. In that competition, George von Elme and Billy Burke tied at 292, then tied the first replay at 149. Burke won the second replay by a single stroke after 72 extra holes.

— MANY WAYS TO PLAY —

There are essentially two main formats in competitive golf: matchplay and strokeplay. In the game's early days, in Scotland, games were always matchplay (ie decided by number of holes won), which was perfectly acceptable when games were played between individuals but could be confusing when societies and larger groups competed for tournaments. In 1754 the Society of St Andrews' Golfers solved this by decreeing that, 'In order to remove all disputes and inconveniences…in all times coming whoever puts in the ball at the fewest strokes over the field shall be declared and sustained victor.' This was the birth of strokeplay.

Strokeplay is now the dominant form of the game, particularly in professional touring golf. Matchplay is considered by many to be the purer form of the game, allowing players more scope to compete against other players with less regard for the standard scratch score of the course. In matchplay all balls are picked up after a hole has been won and the game finishes when a player or team is ahead by more holes than remain on the course. Televised games of golf focus almost exclusively on strokeplay, and matchplay is usually seen only in the Ryder Cup, in the fourball and foursome formats described below. There are, however, many other formats of this type of game, as follows:

FOURBALL
Here, two players form a team, playing against two others. The best scores by each team on each hole count towards the total.

FOURSOMES
Known in the USA as 'alternate shot', this is where two players again form a team but this time play one ball between them in alternate shots. Each player takes turns in driving from the tee, irrespective of who was the last to putt into the previous hole. Many friendships have been ruined by playing to this format.

GREENSOMES
Here both players in a team drive off on every hole and then choose the ball position they prefer. The hole then proceeds as with foursomes.

SKINS

This is a gambling game, played usually in the US, where players compete with each other for money on each hole. If someone wins outright, he or she picks up a skin, while on a tie the money is carried over to the next hole, and so on it goes. At the end of every USPGA Tour season, there is a televised skins game, which usually attracts big TV audiences. In November the Merill Lynch 2004 Skins Game attracted Tiger Woods, Annika Sorenstam, Fred Couples and Adam Scott to compete for $1 million in prize money.

TEXAS SCRAMBLE

Scrambles usually involve four-person teams playing four balls, with each shot coming from the same spot (the best of the four drives is chosen and all four team members then hit from that spot, and so on). In Texas Scramble, at least four drives from each member of the team must be used during the course of the round – ie at least four drives hit by Player A, four by Player B and so on. In a regular scramble, the best driver might well find that his or her tee ball is the one used on every hole. A Texas Scramble prevents that from happening, the rules dictating that even the weakest driver on the team must take his or her four drives. If a scramble is between two teams of three, each player in each team must drive five times.

STABLEFORD

A system invented in 1931 by Dr Frank Stableford from Wallasey, Merseyside, this format is preferred by club golfers and amateurs, as it allows one to have some poor scores on certain holes but to compensate for this with good scores on others. Linked to a player's handicap and to the degree of difficulty of the 18 holes, the format normally gives four points for an eagle, three for a birdie, two for a par, one for a bogey and nothing for a double bogey or worse. Other scoring systems exist, notably at the only large tournament played under Stableford rules: the International at Castle Pines Golf Club in Colorado, which is part of the USPGA Tour. Here, eight points are awarded for an albatross (double eagle), five for an eagle, two for a birdie, nothing for a par, minus one for a bogey and minus three for a double bogey or worse.

— GO, ANNIKA! —

The best woman golfer on the planet, and the US LPGA all-time money winner, caused headlines and controversy in May 2003. Annika Sorenstam, winner of 43 LPGA titles and the only woman to have shot 59 on a Tour event, accepted a sponsor's invitation from the Bank of America to play on the USPGA Tour Colonial tournament with...men.

The Colonial course in Fort Worth, Texas, is known as 'Hogan's Alley', after the great Ben Hogan, who won no less than six times on his home course. A relatively short (7,080-yard), tight course, it was suited to Sorenstam's accurate, long game, although she was driving from the men's championship tees; the 'SuperSwede' regularly hits her drive 265 yards, further than, for instance, Nick Price, who has already won the tournament. It was not, however, technical ability or the sponsor's favouritism that created the furore; rather, it was her sex.

Prior to her appearance at the Colonial, no woman had played on the male PGA Tour since the renowned Babe Zaharias had competed in the 1945 Los Angeles Open. When Sorenstam's appearance was announced, sexism appeared to raise its head, with Vijay Singh opining, 'She doesn't belong out there,' and that she was 'taking a spot from someone else in the field' (ignoring the other seven sponsors' exemptions, which went to men). Singh also stated that he would withdraw if he was selected to play alongside Sorenstam, a statement he later recanted (with his lofty status, he wouldn't have been paired with her anyway). Nick Price also objected, describing the invitation as reeking of publicity (what's that badge on your jersey, Nick? Nike?). Other players, to their credit, spoke up on her behalf. Phil Mickelson said, 'It's not the men's tour; it's the best tour for the best players in the world,' and Gary Player commented, 'We've got to offer the public something exciting.' There was extraordinary public interest in Sorenstam's foray into the men's world, with over 550 accredited reporters attending, more than three times as many as in any previous Tour event.

A clearly nervous Sorenstam missed only one fairway and four greens in her opening-round 71 (one over par), while her second-round 74 – in which she took five bogeys in eight holes – saw her missing the cut and tieing for 96th place. She was in good company; others who missed the cut included Bob Estes (then ranked 16th in the world), Craig Perks (winner of the 2002 Players Championship) and Mark Brooks (1996 PGA Champion). Sorenstam had the courage to take on some of the best golfers in the world and by no means disgraced herself or women's golf. As she left the Colonial, the tearful Swede said, 'This is way over my head. I know where I belong.' The winner, Kenny Perry, commented ruefully, 'I'll probably be remembered as the guy who won Annika's event. That's okay with me. At least I'll be remembered for something.'

— STYMIED —

It's always a shame when an old tradition disappears. Such was the case with the 'stymie', which, having been an accepted part of the game since 1812, was abolished by the R&A and the USGA in 1951. A stymie occurred when a player's route to the pin was blocked by another player's ball, unless the distance involved was of 6in or less, in which case picking up the ball and marking it wasn't an option; the stymied player had either to chip the ball over the obstacle or find a way to the hole by using the contours of the green. One of the most famous examples of the adroit use of a stymie could be seen in Bobby Jones's 19th-hole win over Cyril Tolley in the US Amateur in 1930, on Jones's way to winning the Grand Slam that year.

— ALLISS' HALL OF FAME: BOBBY JONES —

The greatest amateur golfer of all time, Bobby Jones enjoyed only a brief golfing career, but he cast an incomparable record. A qualified engineer and lawyer with a Harvard degree in English literature, he was atypical of most leading golfers but could outplay them in virtually every department of the game.

Early in his career, Jones had to learn to conquer a self-destructive temper on the golf course. Indeed, in 1921 at his first British Open at St Andrews he stormed off the course after shooting a third-round 46 on the front nine. However, between 1923 and 1930, now more equable in temperament, the stocky, Atlanta-born southerner with the elegant swing won five US Amateur, four US Open and three British Open titles, along with one British Amateur win. His list of titles began in 1923 with the US Open, and in 1926 he added further US and UK Open titles, his British win coming at Royal Lytham, and on his return to the States that year he received a ticker-tape welcome in New York City. The following year he won the British Open again, this time at St Andrews by six strokes.

Jones's greatest year, however, was 1930. At that time, the 'Grand Slam' constituted the US and UK Opens and Amateurs, four titles known as the 'Impregnable Quadrilateral'. Impregnable for everyone else up till then, perhaps, but not to Jones, who won the British Amateur at St Andrews by six and seven and a fortnight later won the British Open at Hoylake. There then followed a below-par 287 to win the US Open at Interlachen and, later in the year, victory at the US Amateur at Merion, where he defeated Gene Homans to win by eight and seven.

At the age of 28, Jones retired from competitive golf. In just eight years he had won 13 Majors (a record since exceeded only by Jack Nicklaus), written and developed golf books and films, co-designed Augusta National golf course, was instrumental in founding the Masters and continued to practise law. He later contracted syringomyelia, a painful and disabling spinal disease, which confined him to a wheelchair, and in 1958 he was granted the Freedom of the City of St Andrews. He died in 1971 at the age of 69.

— THE MISSING LINK —

The term 'links' is often used generically to refer to a golf course, particularly in the USA. But are these terms really interchangeable? The word 'links' came into usage in the 15th century at St Andrews, where the 22-hole golf course was referred to as the 'links', but what's the definition of the term?

The *Chambers 20th-Century Dictionary* defines a links as 'a stretch of flat or gently undulating ground along a sea shore, hence a golf course', while in his 1887 book *The Art Of Golf*, Sir Walter Simpson wrote, 'The grounds on which golf is played are called links, being the barren sandy soil from which the sea has retired in recent geological times. In their natural state, links are covered with long, rank bent grass and gorse. Links are too barren for cultivation, but sheep, rabbits, geese and professionals pick up a precarious livelihood on them.'

So, a links course must be beside the sea and unable to be cultivated, with sheep grazing and gorse growing on it. It's difficult to think of any US course with these characteristics, but extract the sheep and there are many such examples in Scotland, from Troon to St Andrews. Indeed, include the sheep and Sir Walter's definition holds true for Scotland's Brora Golf Course, a course in the far north of the country on which a couple of greens sport electric fences to dissuade the local sheep that roam the course from venturing onto the putting surface.

Other prerequisites of a links course include the weather, which must be windy, cold and often wet; the many fiendish and often invisible pot bunkers, occasionally equipped with ladders to provide access to their depths; the fairway terrain, which should be unpredictably bumpy, hilly and entirely unsuited for target golf; the greens, which are often large and difficult to read; and the rough, thick grass and heather, which clutch the ball so tenaciously that the use of a flailing sand wedge is required. All in all, the correct definition of a links is about a million miles from the well-tended, smooth and manicured courses of North America.

— WHEN GOOD GOLFERS GO BAD 1 —

'The least thing upset him on the links. He missed short putts
because of the uproar of butterflies in adjoining meadows.'
— *PG Wodehouse*, The Clickings Of Cuthbert

Golfers all know the feeling. Suddenly the mist descends, the
blood begins to boil and the irrational mind takes over. It's the
Devil's work: golf rage. Some are better than others at dealing
with it, but everyone experiences the sensation at some point.

Many top golfers have, over the years, proven less than
disciplined when things go wrong on the golf course; think
Arnold Palmer, Steve 'Volcano' Pates, young Tiger Woods,
Craig Stadler and Colin Montgomerie, among many others.
Even the saintly Bobby Jones had problems with his temper
as a young man; at the 1921 British Open at St Andrews, he
scored 46 on the front nine, hit his shot at the 11th into a
bunker, took four to get out, ripped up his card and stormed
off the course. At the 1979 Japanese Open, Mark McNulty,
distracted by an annoying fan in the gallery, broke his putter
over his knee and had to putt the rest of the round with his
one-iron. At the 1987 Kemper Open, Greg Norman attempted
to hurl his ball into the water after a bad shot. (It hit his playing
partner, Fred Couples, in the chest.) And after a bad first round
at the 1999 US Open at Pinehurst, José Maria Olazábal
punched his hotel-room wall, broke a bone in his hand and
had to withdraw from the tournament. These, of course, are
only isolated examples; there are many, many more.

The daddy of golf rage, the man with whom the term 'losing
it' is most closely identified, was Tommy Bolt, the 'Vesuvius
of golf'. Known variously as 'Terrible' Tommy and Tommy
'Thunder' Bolt, he was a golfer of considerable talent who
won the 1958 US Open as well as 15 other USPGA events,
but his hair-trigger temperament too often confounded his
abilities. His mentor, Ben Hogan, remarked, 'If I could only
have screwed another head on Tommy's shoulders, he could
have been the greatest player that ever played.' Renowned
for throwing his clubs, at the elite Colonial he flung an iron,
breaking it in half, and there's a famous photograph of Tommy
launching his driver into the lake at the 1960 US Open at

Cherry Hills, having hit his second drive into the water.

Bolt was once on a fairway at Pebble Beach when he asked his caddy for the yardage to the pin. 'One thirty-five,' replied the caddy. 'A soft seven-iron, then?' queried Bolt. 'Gotta be a three-wood or a three-iron,' said the caddy. 'Those are the only clubs you have left.' (Something of a pragmatist, Bolt once commented, 'If you're going to throw a club, it's important to throw it ahead of you so you don't waste your energy going back to pick it up.')

As well as his javelin-like tendencies, Bolt was somewhat unpredictable in his behaviour on the course. At the 1959 Memphis Open, he had a sudden attack of loud flatulence as his opponent was preparing to putt and was fined $250 for 'conduct unbecoming a professional golfer', while at another tournament he marched off the course when he felt that the gallery had not responded positively enough to a shot he considered worthy of greater acclaim.

— WHEN GOOD GOLFERS GO BAD 2 —

In the same league as Tommy Bolt, but considerably more masochistic, was Wilbur Artist 'Lefty' Stackhouse, a wiry Texan touring professional in the 1930s and 1940s. Lefty had a terrible temper, which he mainly visited upon himself. As Sam Snead once commented, 'Lefty'd git so mad at himself he'd bite his own hand.' Some of his tantrums included the following:

- He missed a putt, walked to the edge of the green, hit himself on the chin and knocked himself out;

- He missed a putt on the final green, walked to the nearest tree and started butting his head on the trunk;

- After driving into a water hazard he threw his clubs into the water and dived in head first, following them into the shallow rocky pond;

- After a particularly disastrous round he smashed an entire set of clubs to pieces against a tree trunk;

- After hooking a drive, he walked over to a thorny rose bush and dragged his right hand through it several times, drawing blood – and then did the same with his left hand;

— WHEN GOOD GOLFERS GO BAD 2 (CONT'D) —

- In a money match, he started beating his head against rocks then stopped, threw his wallet on the ground, told his fellow competitors to take out what he owed them in case he killed himself, and went back to beating his head against the rocks.

— WHEN GOOD GOLFERS GO BAD 3 —

A drinking buddy of Lefty was Ky Laffoon, another touring pro and a Cherokee Indian who was Lefty's equal in golfing histrionics. Ky once missed a putt in the final round of an El Paso tournament, tied his putter to his car bumper and drove 600 miles to San Antonio, trailing the errant club behind him. 'The dirty son of a bitch deserved it,' he said.

During the Sacramento Open, Ky missed an easy putt, slammed the putter into his foot and broke not only the club but also his toe.

In another tournament, struggling to get his ball out of a forsythia bush, Ky gave up and started ripping the bush out by its roots. His watching wife, who had given him an ultimatum about his temper, strode off to the car park. Ky ran after her, saying, ' I didn't lose my temper, honey. I just don't like forsythia.' It's not known if this ploy worked.

Finally, at the Jacksonville Open, Ky missed an important putt and threw his putter into a pond, screaming 'Drown, you son of a bitch!' They don't make them like that any more.

— ALLISS' HALL OF FAME: ERNIE ELS —

A big South African who hits the ball a long way but who also possesses a delicate touch around the green and the bunker, Ernie Els is currently one of the best golfers in the world. Known as 'the Big Easy' for his unruffled manner and his languid yet powerful swing, Els has accumulated 15 PGA Tour and 16 European Tour titles and 22 other international victories in his career.

A gifted all-round sportsman, Els chose to focus on golf at the age of 14. He missed the cut in the British Open in 1989, but three years later in 1992 he won the South African Open, PGA and Masters, the first golfer to do so since Gary Player ten years earlier. His first win on the European Tour was the 1994 Dubai Classic, and in the same year he claimed his first Major, the US Open, beating Colin Montgomerie and Loren Roberts in a playoff at Oakmont and becoming only the second South African golfer after Gary Player to win the title. His first win on the US Tour came the following year at the Byron Nelson Classic, and in 1997 he won the US Open again, this time beating Colin Montgomerie by one stroke at Congressional.

2000 was a year of almosts for Ernie, a year in which he became the first golfer to finish in second place in three consecutive Majors, runner-up to Vijay Singh in the Masters and to Tiger Woods in the US and British Opens. He atoned for this in 2002, when he won the Open at Muirfield in a sudden-death playoff with Thomas Levet, chipping from a difficult lie in a greenside bunker to within 5ft to secure the title on the first playoff hole. The following year he won the first two tournaments in the US Tour, and his four wins in the European Tour drove him to the top of the Order of Merit.

In 2004, his performances on the European Tour saw him retain the Order of Merit, and he repeated his second consecutive hat-trick in the World Matchplay Championship, having previously won three times in succession between 1994 and 1996, while his three wins in the USA helped him to second place in the World Golf rankings, behind a rejuvenated Vijay Singh and ahead of Tiger Woods. The Big Easy appears to have several more victories ahead of him.

— FOUR GREAT GOLF COLLAPSES —

Elsewhere in this book is a reference to Greg Norman's collapse to Nick Faldo in the final round of the 1996 Masters. Here are some more examples of golfers throwing away apparently unassailable leads.

1966 US OPEN, OLYMPIC CLUB

Arnold Palmer's aggressive style of play saw him seven shots ahead of Billy Caspar with nine to play in the final round. Perhaps distracted by the thought of beating Ben Hogan's US Open record of 276 (level par on the back nine would give him a total of 274), he failed to protect his lead. By the 13th, he was five ahead. At the short 15th he took a four, Caspar putted for a two and the lead was now three strokes. A wild tee shot at the 16th resulted in a six for Palmer, while Caspar scored four, leaving Palmer one ahead with two to play. At the difficult 17th, Palmer again drove into the rough and the match was all square. Both men parred the 18th, leading to a playoff that Caspar won by 69 to 73.

1999 BRITISH OPEN, CARNOUSTIE

Frenchman Jean Van de Velde reached the final hole of the tournament with a three-stroke lead over Paul Lawrie and Justin Leonard. Needing only a two-over-par six to win, the Frenchman contrived a farcical finish. Instead of opting for the safety of an iron, Van de Velde reached for his driver and hit his tee shot to the right, onto the 17th fairway. Caution not being part of his make-up, he hit his second shot in the direction of a blind green instead of laying up, and the ball bounced off a stanchion into the rough 30 yards from the green. He chipped his third shot into the Barry Burn, with its deep concrete walls, took off his shoes and socks and walked into the burn, but then changed his mind, instead taking a penalty drop into the rough. After mishitting what was now his fifth shot into a greenside bunker, his sixth landed six feet from the pin and he putted in for a seven and a three-way playoff with Paul Lawrie and Justin Leonard. After this stunning piece of self-destruction, Van de Velde proceeded to lose to Lawrie, who had started the final round ten strokes off the lead and became the first Scotsman to win on Scottish soil for 68 years.

2000 AT&T PRO-AM, PEBBLE BEACH, CALIFORNIA

Rookie Matt Gogel held the lead in the final round of this weather-affected tournament, shooting three birdies at the start. By the time Tiger Woods teed off on the 12th, Gogel was seven shots ahead and playing three groups behind Woods, who birdied the 12th and parred the 13th and 14th. On the 15th Woods hit his approach shot from 100 yards and the ball landed 3ft from the pin and rolled in to the cup for a magnificent eagle. His approach at the next hole was from 114 yards and was almost as sensational as his previous hole, the ball landing 2ft from the pin – another birdie. Tiger then parred the 17th and birdied the 18th for a final score of 64. Meanwhile, Gogel had bogeyed the 11th, 12th and 15th and would take 40 for the back nine. Tiger's eagle-birdie-par-birdie finish had won him the tournament. Gogel said afterwards of Woods' performance, 'I was amazed. I will never be amazed again.'

1939 US OPEN, PHILADELPHIA COUNTRY CLUB

'Slammin'' Sam Snead never won the US Open, but he could have, had he not miscalculated in the 1939 tournament. Playing an hour ahead of his closest contenders, Snead reached the 18th and final hole of the tournament. This was in the days before scoreboards were erected on courses, and Snead felt that he had to score a birdie on the last to be sure of winning. In fact, all he needed was a par. However, he ripped into his drive off the 18th tee and found the rough. He hit with another wood for his second but it reached only as far as a fairway bunker 100 yards from the green. His third shot lipped the bunker but remained in the sand, and his fourth went over the green into the gallery. He chipped onto the green and three-putted for an eight, ruling himself out of the three-way playoff between Craig Wood, Denny Shute and Byron Nelson, which Nelson won. Snead remarked later, 'I wouldn't have hit so dumb a second shot, but I didn't know I didn't need a birdie so badly.'

— THE TRAP —

The world's largest bunker is Hell's Half Acre, on the 585-yard seventh hole of the Pine Valley Course in New Jersey.

— RULES OF ENGAGEMENT —

Many golf clubs have local rules that take in the various hazards around the course. For pragmatism and sheer English determination to play on whatever the situation, however, few can match the rules established by Richmond Golf Club in 1940, during the Second World War, which ran as follows:

1. Players are asked to collect bomb and shrapnel splinters to save these causing damage to the mowing machines.

2. In competitions during gunfire or while bombs are falling, players may take cover without penalty for ceasing play.

3. The position of delayed-action bombs are marked by red flags at reasonable distance, but not guaranteed same distance therefrom.

4. Shrapnel or bomb splinters on the fairway or in bunkers, within a club's length of the ball, may be moved without penalty.

5. A ball moved, or lost, by enemy action may be replaced by a new ball without penalty.

6. A ball lying in a bomb crater may be lifted and dropped not nearer the hole, preserving the line to the hole, without penalty.

7. A player whose stroke is affected by the simultaneous explosion of a bomb may play another ball from the same place. Penalty: one stroke.

— THE GREAT BATTLES OF GOLF HISTORY 2 —

TONY JACKLIN V LEE TREVINO, BRITISH OPEN, MUIRFIELD, 1972
Tony Jacklin might have been the 1969 British Open champion, but the favourite at Muirfield was Jack Nicklaus, intent on winning the tournament to equal Ben Hogan's treble of three Majors in one season. However, it was another British Open winner, 'Supermex' Lee Trevino, who set the pace at the famous old Scottish links.

A typically buccaneering 66 from Trevino and a splendidly paced 67 from Jacklin in the third round saw the American lead the Englishman by one shot, with Nicklaus struggling six shots behind. The leading pair were neck and neck on the last round until the par-five 17th hole, which required a long drive and a second accurate shot between the traps guarding the green. Jacklin chipped weakly onto the green for three while Trevino's fourth was in some rough behind the putting surface. Trevino, with the honour, chipped into the hole to make par. This was a crucial psychological moment for Jacklin, who then three-putted, his nerve broken.

Another bogey by Jacklin at the last hole gave the title to Trevino, while a late charge from Nicklaus relegated a devastated Jacklin to third place. Trevino, with 278, had set a new course record for Muirfield.

— THE WORLD'S TEN GREATEST HOLES —

1. ST ANDREWS, 17TH, FIFE, SCOTLAND

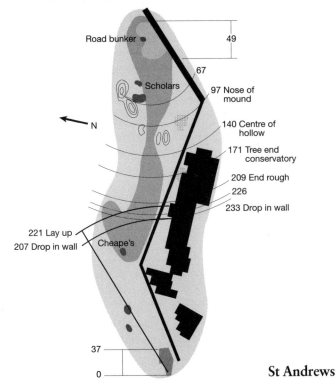

St Andrews

— THE WORLD'S TEN GREATEST HOLES (CONT'D) —

The famous 17th hole at St Andrews, nicknamed the 'Road Hole', is commonly regarded as one of the hardest par fours in world golf. At 461 yards, it's not particularly long, but it has destroyed many illustrious cards in its time. The tee shot has to carry a hotel on the right, with a slight draw, yet not go too far into the thick rough, while the second shot has to land on the relatively narrow green, with a deep pot bunker in front and a road immediately behind. The alternative is to aim at the 18th tee or lay up, but bogeys beckon these shots.

The Road Hole has claimed many scalps, including five-time British Open winner JH Taylor, who took 13 strokes to emerge from the bunker in 1921; Tommy Nakajima, who took five in the 1978 British Open and after whom the bunker was referred to as 'the Sands of Nakajima' (Nakajima had earlier that year taken 13 on the 13th hole at Augusta in the Masters, the highest ever score on one hole in the Masters); Tom Watson, whose attempt to equal Harry Vardon's record of six British Open wins was denied by his ball running onto the road and lodging beside a wall; Costantino Rocca, who took three to extricate himself from the bunker and lose the 1995 British Open playoff to John Daly; and David Duval, whose four attempts from the sand in the 2000 British Open saw him drop from second to tied 11th.

The bunker has been altered for the 2005 British Open but its height and steepness remain. The St Andrews authorities state that 'The Road Hole bunker will retain its fearsome reputation and prove even more of a challenge to the world's best golfers.'

2. CYPRESS POINT, 16TH, MONTEREY, CALIFORNIA
One of the most beautiful holes in the world, this 231-yard par three is also one of the most difficult. Situated in Pebble Beach, California, the course was designed by Alister Mackenzie, the architect of the course at Augusta, and has been described as the Sistine Chapel of golf. The 16th tee stands above the ocean, the green is guarded by bunkers and beyond the Pacific stretches to the horizon. The hole demands a full carry over the surf and the rocks, and a par is famously difficult to achieve, even with a driver.

The fairway stretches to the left and, with safety in mind, many experienced players aim there with a view to a bogey and a thankful walk to the neighbouring 17th tee. Bing Crosby, who was one of the progenitors of the National Pro-Am tournament (now sponsored by AT&T), once played here and is one of only four golfers to have aced this hole. Groucho Marx, however, was not so fortunate; he once hit his first five tee shots into the water on the 16th, threw his clubs into the ocean and resolved never again to play the game.

The Cypress Point 16th hole combines spectacular beauty with sheer difficulty, exacerbated by the constantly changing wind, and many members of the USPGA are somewhat relieved that the course is no longer part of the Tour.

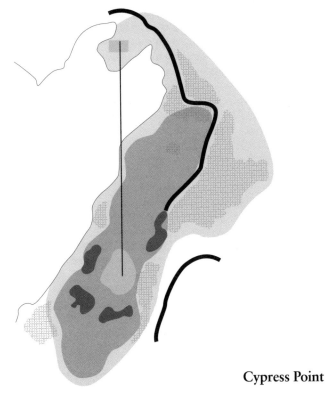

Cypress Point

3.   ROYAL TROON, EIGHTH, AYRSHIRE, SCOTLAND
    At 126 yards, this is the shortest hole in Open Championship golf. With its tiny green guarded by deep bunkers, it was originally known as 'Ailsa', for the view of Ailsa Crag in the distance. Willie Park, writing in *Golf*

— THE WORLD'S TEN GREATEST HOLES (CONT'D) —

Illustrated, described it as 'a pitching surface trimmed down to the size of a postage stamp', and since then it's been known as the 'Postage Stamp'.

The eighth hole has crushed the spirit of many golfers, notably the unfortunate amateur Herman Tissies, who scraped a 15 in the 1950 British Open, and Tiger Woods, who triple-bogeyed it in 1997. In 1982, playing alongside former British Open champions Max Faulkner and Fred Daly, 71-year-old Gene Sarazen celebrated the 50th anniversary of his British Open win by holing in one with a five-iron. The following day, his tee shot found the deep bunker on the right. Using a sand wedge – his own invention – Sarazen chipped in for a birdie. A newspaper the following day led its sports coverage with the headline 'Sarazen licks Postage Stamp'.

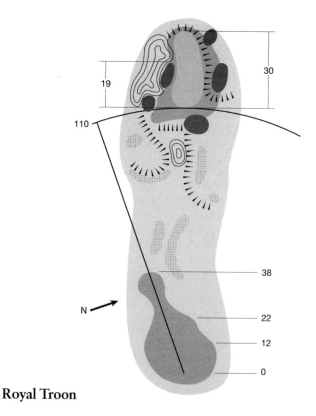

Royal Troon

4. SAWGRASS, 17TH, PONTE VEDRA, FLORIDA

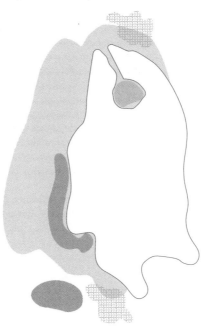

Sawgrass

Home to the Players Championship and located next to USPGA Tour headquarters, Sawgrass is the US's first stadium golf course and its construction heralded the era of 'target golf'. The course was bought for $1 and designed by Pete Dye from 400 acres of swamp. Its signature hole is the 17th, which features an island-green par three with a length of 132 yards.

The Sawgrass 17th hole is probably the most famous on the US Tour and has been responsible for destroying many scores at the annual Players. Sawgrass is also a public, resort course, and it has been estimated that between 120,000 and 150,000 balls are recovered each year from the lake around the 17th. Players are divided in their opinions of the hole, with Fred Couples (who once sent his tee shot into the water and holed with his next shot) stating, 'It's the best hole on Tour,' while Lee Janzen observed, 'Some of us love to hate it.' Darren Clarke summed up most players' feelings by saying, 'Close your eyes and hit it quick.'

— THE WORLD'S TEN GREATEST HOLES (CONT'D) —

The highest score on the Sawgrass 17th in the Players tournament was 11, hit by Robert Gamez in 1990, while Len Mattiace, one stroke behind leader Justin Leonard in 1998, took an eight. During one windy opening round in 1984, 64 balls ended up in the water. Although not the most difficult hole at Sawgrass, the position of the 17th as the penultimate hole fills pros with dread. You haven't won 'til you've got past 17.

5. AUGUSTA NATIONAL, 12TH, AUGUSTA, GEORGIA
    Known as 'Golden Bell', the par-three, 155-yard 12th hole at Augusta is one of the three holes that constitute 'Amen Corner'. Described by Jack Nicklaus as 'the most demanding tournament hole in the world', the Augusta 12th requires an accurate tee shot over Rae's Creek onto a narrow green, defended at front and rear by bunkers. The second-toughest hole on the course after the tenth, the difficulty of the hole is compounded by the swirling, undecipherable winds that sweep down from the adjacent tall pines. With regard to the hole, Ben Hogan – who has a bridge over Rae's Creek named in his honour – once advised, 'Never hit until you feel the wind on your cheek.'

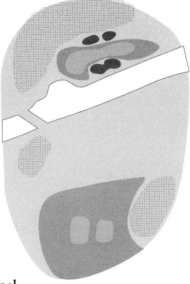

Augusta National

The highest score on the Augusta 12th in the Masters came in 1980 when Tom Weiskopf scored a 13, and the same hole saw Nick Faldo take the lead in 1996 when Greg Norman double-bogeyed and Faldo parred. Controversy occurred in 1958 when, in the final round of the Masters, Arnold Palmer embedded a tee shot into the rain-soaked back of the green and claimed relief. He was denied this and double-bogeyed. He then dropped a ball at the same spot and parred. When his round ended, the denial of relief was overturned and his par score stood, and Palmer went on to win the tournament by two strokes. To this day, his playing partner Ken Venturi (who ended two strokes behind Palmer) claimed that Palmer hadn't nominated a second ball until shooting his double bogey, a clear infringement of the rules that Palmer has always denied.

6. **PEBBLE BEACH, EIGHTH, MONTEREY, CALIFORNIA**

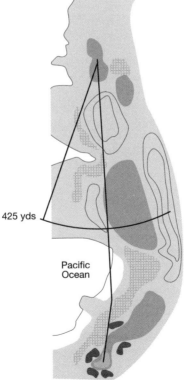

425 yds

Pacific
Ocean

Pebble Beach

— THE WORLD'S TEN GREATEST HOLES (CONT'D) —

One of the most spectacular golf courses in the world, set alongside the Pacific Ocean, the Pebble Beach course contains some extremely testing holes, notably the short seventh, whose green nestles just beside the ocean, and the magnificent par-five 18th, which curls alongside the shoreline. The eighth, however, is particularly memorable.

A 425-yard par four, the Pebble Beach eighth hole requires a blind uphill drive on a rollercoaster fairway adjacent to the cliffs and ocean. The second shot – described by Jack Nicklaus as the 'greatest second shot in the game' – needs a carry of around 170 yards across the ocean towards a green protected by bunkers on three sides. The more faint-hearted can aim left and hit the fairway in an attempt to get on the green in three.

There is a story (officially denied by the club) that a tipsy Japanese golfer died after he drove his golf cart over the cliff on the eighth fairway, which some of the local caddies still call 'Kamikaze Cove'.

7. **VALDERRAMA, 17TH, ANDALUCÍA, SPAIN**

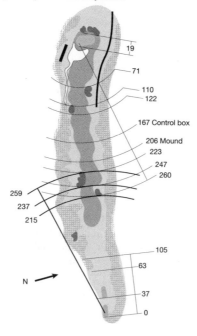

Valderrama

The first European mainland course to be used for the Ryder Cup (in 1997), Valderrama, situated between Málaga and Cádiz, is a tough, demanding parkland course whose most difficult and controversial hole is 'Los Gabiones', the 17th.

Redesigned by Seve Ballesteros, the Valderrama 17th is a 536-yard par five, with a band of rough at approximately the 280-yard mark, thereby limiting the length of the drive. The green is protected to the front by a lake and slopes towards the water, while bunkers protect it to the rear. The second shot is crucial: do you go for the green and risk the water and the bunkers, or do you lay up? The hole is disliked by many pros, including Colin Montgomerie, who once gritted, 'I hate that hole,' and Hal Sutton, who described it as 'pitiful'.

The hole has taken many casualties. In 1997 Tiger Woods putted into the water in the Ryder Cup; in 1999 Woods won the American Express Championship, despite taking an eight at the 17th in the final round; in 2000 Nick Price was one stroke behind Mike Weir in the Volvo Masters and destroyed his chances with an eight at the 17th; and Darren Clarke, in the lead on the second day of the 2004 Volvo Masters, took an 11. 'It's not a very well-designed hole,' said Woods, with some justification.

8. PINE VALLEY, SEVENTH, NEW JERSEY

Designed out of sand dunes and scrub by amateur architect George Crumb in 1912, Pine Valley in New Jersey is considered one of the best, and certainly one of the most difficult, courses in the USA.

The seventh hole, a 585-yard par five, is one of the hardest in the world, and its bunker – the world's largest, known as 'Hell's Half Acre' – begins 285 yards from the tee, bisecting the fairway for another 100 yards and putting pressure on both the drive and the second shot. The green, meanwhile, is virtually imprisoned in a huge bunker. It is virtually impossible to score a birdie on the Pine Valley seventh hole.

9. FIRESTONE SOUTH, 16TH, AKRON, OHIO

Redesigned by Robert Trent Jones in the late 1950s, the Firestone course is currently home to the WGC NEC Invitational. Its par-five 16th hole, originally 625 yards and recently increased to 667, is currently the longest on the PGA Tour. A dogleg with a small green with a pond in front and bunkers behind, it is virtually impossible for all but the longest hitters to hit the green in two. It was christened 'the Monster' by Arnold Palmer in

— THE WORLD'S TEN GREATEST HOLES (CONT'D) —

Pine Valley

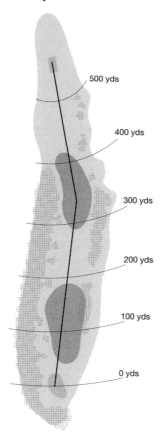

500 yds

400 yds

300 yds

200 yds

100 yds

0 yds

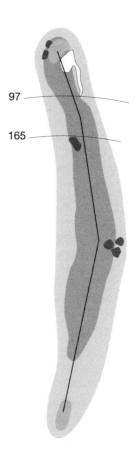

97

165

Firestone South

the 1960 USPGA Championship when he took an eight and ruled himself out of contention. When he took the same score again in 2002 in the Seniors' Tour, he commented, 'That hole has been haunting me for 45 years.'

Not all top golfers have been so unfortunate on the 16th. It was here that Jack Nicklaus, five strokes behind Bruce Crampton in the 1975 USPGA, parred the hole to set up a four-stroke victory.

10. THE BELFRY, 18TH, WEST MIDLANDS, ENGLAND

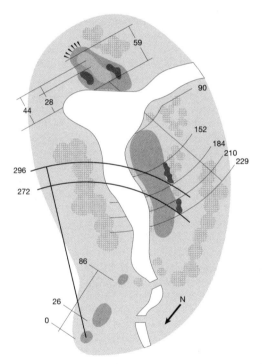

The Belfry

Home to the PGA and host to four Ryder Cup tournaments, the Brabazon Course at the Belfry is a parkland course dotted with streams and lakes, and its 18th hole is one of the most dramatic finishing holes in golf. A left-dogleg, 473-yard par four with a three-tier green guarded by water, it has been the scene of some memorable finishes in the Ryder Cup.

The ideal shot from the tee is long and left over the first water hazard, leaving a second, short shot onto the green over more water. Few who saw it can forget Christy O'Connor's superb two-iron shot to the pin to beat Fred Couples at the final round in 1985, or Sam Torrance's jubilant celebration on the final hole after his birdie putt clinched the trophy for Europe the same year. Likewise, Paul McGinley aced a 10ft putt on the 18th to give Europe the half-point it needed to win in 2002, before he was rewarded with a ducking in the pond.

Perhaps scenically the Belfry is rather dull, but some of golf's most exciting moments have occurred on this Sutton Coldfield course.

— COULDA BEEN A CONTENDER —

Commentators' hyperbole notwithstanding, one isn't always *born* a golfer. Here's a brief list of players who could have made the big time in other sports:

- **Paul McGinley** – A promising Gaelic football midfielder in Ireland who had to retire through injury at the age of 19.

- **Hale Irwin** – A defensive full-back in the University of Colorado's football team.

- **Lucas Parsons** – Won three state high-diving championships in Queensland and was runner-up at the national level.

- **JC Snead** – The nephew of 'Slammin' Sam', winner of eight USPGA titles, played professional baseball for three years.

- **Charles Coody** – The winner of the 1971 Masters played basketball for Texas.

- **Ellsworth Vines** – A US Tour member in the 1940s who also won the 1939 US Tennis Open.

- **Esteban Toledo** – A professional boxer before joining the USPGA Tour.

- **'Jumbo' Ozaki** – 'The Tower' was once a professional baseball player in Japan.

— THE MASTERS TIMELINE: —
DRAMATIC FINISHES

The youngest Major of the four, the Masters was the brainchild of Bobby Jones and Clifford Roberts, who hired renowned golf architect Dr Alister MacKenzie – designer of California course Cypress Point – to convert a Georgia nursery known as 'Fruitlands' into a 365-acre golf course: Augusta National.

Very different in feel to the other Majors, the Masters prides itself on its dignity and exclusiveness. Unlike the three other peripatetic tournaments, the Masters is held every April only at Augusta National, a beautiful, tree-lined, undulating golf course where the holes are all named after blossoms: redwood, magnolia, etc. The fairways are broad and there is little rough, but the greens are lightning-fast and the smooth appearance of the course is deceptive. As Jones once remarked, 'There isn't a hole out there that can't be birdied if you just think, but there isn't one that can't be double-bogeyed if you stop thinking.'

At the Masters, billboards and advertising are conspicuous by their absence and CBS is allowed to air only three advertisements per hour, while television coverage is banned on the first nine holes and tickets for the event are at a premium. All winners receive a green jacket that is available only to them and the club members and that must not be used outside the club for purposes of advertising. The club and the tournament have occasionally been criticised as being autocratic and even reactionary in their attitudes, but the allure of the Masters is impossible to resist.

The following timeline describes the evolution of this most prestigious event on the golfing calendar:

1934   The first Augusta National Invitational. Bobby Jones is lured out of retirement to play and finishes tenth. The tournament is won by Horton Smith.

1935   Gene Sarazen, who missed the first tournament, hits 'the shot heard around the world' and wins after a playoff. The event is now informally known as 'the Masters'.

1942   Byron Nelson wins his second Masters after an 18-hole playoff against Ben Hogan. Nelson shoots five

— THE MASTERS TIMELINE (CONT'D) —

birdies on the last 13 holes to beat Hogan by one shot. The tournament is suspended due to US involvement in World War II.

1949 Sam Snead becomes the first winner to be awarded the green jacket, which until this time had been worn only by members of the club. He finishes with two 67s, his last round containing eight birdies.

1951 Ben Hogan wins his first Masters. The Champions' dinner is instituted, taking place on the Tuesday before the start of the tournament, with the menu chosen by the previous year's champion.

1954 Hogan and Snead play off for the title, which Snead wins – his third – by one stroke.

1956 The Masters receives its first TV broadcast (holes 15–18). Amateur Ken Venturi is ahead after three rounds but shoots 80 on the last day, ultimately losing by one shot.

1958 Arnold Palmer wins his first Major by one stroke.

1959 Art Wall birdies five of the last six holes to win.

1960 Palmer wins again, sinking a 5ft putt on the last hole to beat Venturi.

1961 An over-confident Palmer double-bogeys the last hole to lose to Gary Player, who becomes the first non-American winner of the Masters. Amateur Charles R Coe Jr finishes tied second with Palmer.

1962 Palmer defeats Dow Finsterwald and Player in a final playoff.

1963 Jack Nicklaus wins his first Masters one shot ahead of Tony Lema.

1977 Tom Watson beats Nicklaus by one stroke, despite Nicklaus's last-round 66.

1986 Nicklaus wins his sixth Masters at the age of 46, shooting 65 – including five birdies on the last nine – to see off Ballesteros, Greg Norman and Tom Kite.

1987 Larry Mize dramatically chips in from 140ft on the second playoff hole to beat Greg Norman.

1988 The tournament's third European winner, Sandy Lyle, hits the ball from the bunker on the 18th fairway, 150 yards from the hole, to within 8ft of the pin, and then birdies to beat Mark Calcavecchia by one stroke.

1989 Nick Faldo goes to the playoff against Scott Hoch, who misses a 2ft putt to win on the first extra hole. Faldo then birdies his second extra hole to become the tournament's fourth European winner.

1990 Faldo successfully defends his title, beating Ray Floyd on his second extra playoff hole.

1991 Ian Woosnam birdies the last hole to win the title.

1998 Mark O'Meara birdies his last two holes to win his only Masters.

1999 José Maria Olazábal wins the tournament for the second time.

2003 Mike Weir becomes the first Canadian and first left-hander to win the title at the first playoff hole.

2004 Phil Mickelson breaks his Majors duck to win the title with a final-hole birdie putt to beat Els by one stroke.

— TEN ESSENTIAL FACTS ABOUT THE HOLE IN ONE —

Scoring a hole in one is perhaps the only occasion in sport when the winner buys drinks for the losers. If you're a top professional, the odds against hitting one are approximately 3,700 to 1, whereas for an average player the odds soar to 42,500 to 1. Here are some facts about the 'ace':

— TEN ESSENTIAL FACTS ABOUT THE HOLE IN ONE —
(CONT'D)

1 The earliest recorded hole in one was played at the 1868 British Open Championship, when Tom Morris (Young Tom) performed the feat at the 145-yard eighth hole at Prestwick to win the first of four successive British Open Championships.

2 John Hudson, a 25-year-old professional, holed two consecutive holes in one at the 11th and 12th holes (195 yards and 311 yards, respectively) in the 1971 Martini Tournament at the UK's Royal Norwich course.

3 The longest hole in one was hit by Robert Mitera on 7 October 1965 at the aptly-named Miracle Hills Golf Club in Omaha, Nebraska, when Mitera used his driver to ace the tenth hole from a whopping 444 yards. He couldn't even see the flag from where he teed off and hadn't realised what he'd done until he arrived at the green, whereupon another golfer told him his ball was in the hole.

4 Mrs Argea Tissies, whose husband, Herman, took 15 at Royal Troon's eighth hole, the Postage Stamp, in the 1950 British Open, scored an ace at the second hole at Italy's Punta Ala course in the second round of the 1978 British Ladies' Seniors' Open. Bizarrely, she did it again exactly five years later, on the same date, at the same time of day, in the same round of the same tournament, at the same hole and with the same club.

5 In less than two hours' play in the second round of the 1989 US Open at Oak Hill Country Club, Rochester, New York, four golfers – Doug Weaver, Mark Wiebe, Jerry Pate and Nick Price – each holed the 167-yard sixth hole in one. The odds against four professionals achieving such a record in a field of 156 were calculated as 332,000 to 1.

6 When it comes to young aces, Tiger Woods was just six years old when he hit his first hole in one, while Michelle Wie has had six in her short golfing career after shooting her first at the age of 12. The youngest recorded hole in one, however, appears to be played by Matthew Draper, who, as a five-year-old, aced the 122-yard fourth hole at Cherwell Edge, Oxfordshire.

The oldest player to hit a hole in one is Florida's Harold Stilson, who was 101 years old when he aced the 108-yard 16th hole at the Deerfield Country Club with a four iron in 2001.

At a tournament in Hunstanton, England, in 1974, Bob Taylor holed in one during practice on the 188-yard 16th hole. In the first round, he did it again on the same hole. In the second round, unbelievably, he aced the same hole. The odds against such a performance must be virtually incalculable.

The greatest number of holes in one have been achieved by Californian Norman Manley, who has scored an unbelievable 59 aces, his first coming in 1964. He achieved four in 1979 alone.

While playing with the England football team at Mill Ride in May 1999, British golf journalist Derek Lawrenson holed out in one at the 15th and won a £180,000 Ferrari Diablo. He immediately sold the car and was stripped of his amateur status by the R&A.

— WHAT A STUPID... —

The popular Argentinian golfer Roberto de Vicenzo entered the 1968 Masters having won the British Open the previous year. On the final day of the tournament, Bob Goalby had shot a 66 and de Vicenzo, who had birdied the 17th, needed a par at the 18th to force a playoff. This he duly did and then signed his scorecard, which had been compiled over the round by his playing partner, Tommy Aaron, who had mistakenly put de Vicenzo down for a four instead of a three at the 17th. When he signed the card, de Vicenzo didn't notice this error, and when he finally did, it was too late. Under the rules of golf, he was penalised one shot and Goalby won the Masters by one stroke. 'What a stupid I am,' de Vicenzo was later heard to remark.

— ENDURANCE GOLF 3 —

The longest holed putts in a major tournament were both of 110ft, by Jack Nicklaus in the 1964 Tournament of Champions and Nick Price in the 1992 USPGA. Bobby Jones was also reputed to have holed a putt in excess of 100ft, at the fifth green in the first round of the 1927 British Open at St Andrews.

— ALLISS' HALL OF FAME: GARY PLAYER —

The son of a South African mining engineer, in the 1960s Gary Player developed into one of the best golfers in the world, striding the international golfing stage alongside Palmer and Nicklaus.

Although slight in stature and relatively short off the tee, Player's determination, devotion to physical fitness and deadly short game – particularly from the bunker – brought him over 160 title wins across the world, including 21 US Tours and a career Grand Slam in the Majors. A dedicated practiser of the game, he once famously responded to jibes about being lucky by saying, 'The more I practise, the luckier I get.'

Player's first Major victory was at the 1959 British Open, where after ten solid days of practice at Muirfield he finished with a 68 to clinch the title. He won the British Open again in 1968, at Carnoustie, defeating Nicklaus and Bob Charles by two strokes, and again in 1974 at a windy Royal Lytham, defeating Peter Oosterhuis by four shots. He also won three Masters, his first in 1961, when he became the first non-American to wear the green jacket, and his second in 1974. In 1978, at the age of 42, when he was seven shots behind leader Hubert Green at the beginning of the last round at Augusta, he shot a magnificent 30, including six birdies, on the back nine to claim victory for the third time.

In 1962 Player held off Bob Goalby to win the USPGA title by one shot before winning a second time in 1972, coping well with anti-apartheid, pro-civil-rights demonstrations aimed against him. In his later years, Player recanted his earlier pro-apartheid beliefs, stating that he was naïve in his judgement.

The South African's career Grand Slam was completed in 1965 when he threw away the lead with three holes to go at Bellerive, St Louis, by triple-bogeying the 70th hole, thus allowing Kel Nagle into an 18-hole playoff that Player won by three strokes.

Perhaps Player's favourite event, however, was the World Matchplay Championship, which he won five times between 1965 and 1973. In recent years, he has played on the US Seniors' Tour, where he has won six major titles and collected well in advance of £5 million. He currently runs a number of international businesses, including a stud farm and a company that designs golf-course architecture, and he set up the Gary Player Foundation to promote education in South Africa.

— GOLF'S LORD BYRON —

Along with Sam Snead and Ben Hogan, 'Lord' Byron Nelson was one of the leading golfing triumvirate of the 1940s. A Texan, Nelson had already won the Masters in 1937 and 1942, the US Open in 1939 and the USPGA in 1940 and 1945. He tried to enlist for the Second World War in 1942 but a blood condition ruled him out of service, so he teamed up with fellow rejectee Harold 'Jug' McSpadden, and the pair – known as the Gold Dust Twins – played over 100 exhibition matches in aid of the war effort.

In 1945, Nelson set a record that's unlikely ever to be broken when he won 18 tournaments – including an amazing 11 in succession – on the USA Tour, playing 19 consecutive rounds under 70 that season and averaging 68.33, earning him the moniker 'the Streak'. He commented, 'My game had gotten so good and dependable that there were times when I would actually get bored playing.' His career total of 52 official Tour wins places him fifth in the all-time winning list. He retired at the early age of 34 in 1946.

Nelson's sequence in 1945 has been disparaged by some critics on the grounds that in that year the Tour had been depleted due to the fact that many top professionals – including his Texan childhood friend and rival Hogan – were

— GOLF'S LORD BYRON (CONT'D) —

still in military service. However, the strokeplay statistics in 1945 speak for themselves and confirm Nelson as one of the true greats of the game.

Nelson was also the model for the Iron Byron, a machine developed in 1966 that replicated his swing and is still in use today to test golf equipment. The Byron Nelson Classic has been a staple of the US Tour since 1968, and the old man is an official starter at the Masters every year.

— A POTTED HISTORY OF THE RYDER CUP —

There are few sporting occasions that match the biennial Ryder Cup for excitement and edge-of-seat tension. As well as providing dramatic viewing for the spectator, the tournament gives the players an opportunity to depart from their isolated, individual grind on the Tours and become part of a team, with communal responsibilities and the rare chance to develop an *esprit de corps*. Furthermore, their golf is tested over the three days in the different formats of fourball, foursomes and singles. It's little wonder that the top golfers desperately compete for selection in the teams, even though they're not paid. In the words of Gene Sarazen, 'You have to remember that the Ryder Cup was the players' idea. It came from them.'

The present arrangement, in which 12 players from Europe compete against 12 from the USA, began in 1979 and replaced the pre-existing USA v Great Britain and Ireland competition, which had been held since 1927, when the trophy was originally donated by English seed merchant Samuel Ryder. The 13th member of each team is the non-playing captain, who decides who accompanies whom in the foursomes and fourballs and the order in which players compete in the singles match, which is always played on the last day. The tournament alternates between the two continents every other year.

Under the old format, the US won 19, Great Britain and Ireland three and one match was drawn. Captain Ben Hogan's sides inflicted the heaviest defeats on GB&I (Great Britain and Ireland) at Portland, Oregon (11–1), in 1947 and at Houston, Texas (23.5–8.5), in 1967. Dai Rees was GB&I captain for the latter tournament, but he was also in charge ten years earlier when GB&I ran up their best score against the US: 7.5–4.5 at Lindrick, Nottinghamshire. In 1977, after a US 12.5–7.5 win at Royal Lytham, Jack Nicklaus suggested to Lord

Derby, President of the PGA, that the contest might become more equal and retain its prestige if a European select was chosen rather than simply GB&I. An initially reluctant PGA eventually saw the wisdom of Nicklaus's suggestion, and the first match in the new series took place in 1979. Here's a brief summary of the tournaments that have taken place since then:

1979, THE GREENBRIER, WEST VIRGINIA
CAPTAINS: BILLY CASPER (US), JOHN JACOBS (EUROPE)
Seve Ballesteros and Antonio Garrido were the first Europeans to play in the new Ryder Cup, although their partnership resulted in only one win out of four and both lost their singles matches. All 12 players competed in the final-day singles math (prior to this, there had been only ten singles), and by the halfway stage the US had won five out of six, which proved to be the final winning margin. On their return to the UK, Mark James and Ken Brown were heavily fined for their childish behaviour at the tournament.

Result: USA 17, Europe 11

1981, WALTON HEATH, SURREY
CAPTAINS: JOHN JACOBS (EUROPE), DAVE MARR (USA)
Jacobs' team fielded three new players – Manuel Pinero, José Maria Canizares and Bernhard Langer – but the Europeans were no match for a supremely talented US line-up featuring such luminaries as Jack Nicklaus, Tom Watson, Lee Trevino, Hale Irwin and Tom Kite. (Surprisingly, Ballesteros and Tony Jacklin had been dropped by Europe.) The visitors managed wins in only two of the eight foursomes and three out of the eight fourballs. Nick Faldo did beat Johnny Miller 2&1 in the singles, but Europe were outclassed.

Result: USA 18.5, Europe 9.5

1983, PGA NATIONAL, PALM BEACH, FLORIDA
CAPTAINS: TONY JACKLIN (EUROPE), JACK NICKLAUS (USA)
New captain Jacklin decided to introduce some professionalism into the European side and flew the team over by Concorde. A re-energised Ballesteros was back and by the end of the second day Europe were level with the USA. In the singles, Ballesteros played a magnificent three-wood 240 yards from a bunker on the 18th to snatch a half from Fuzzy Zoeller, and the lead then zigzagged between the two teams. With two matches left, Lanny Wadkins, one down against José

— A POTTED HISTORY OF THE RYDER CUP (CONT'D) —

Maria Canizares on the 18th, rescued a half with a beautifully judged
wedge shot, while Tom Watson's bogey four on the 17th claimed the
match from Bernard Gallacher, who took a double bogey. That was
enough for the US to retain the Ryder Cup, Europe were narrowly
beaten but far from disgraced.

Result USA 14.5, Europe 13.5

1985, THE BELFRY, WEST MIDLANDS
CAPTAINS: TONY JACKLIN (EUROPE), LEE TREVINO (USA)
This year's home side featured five continentals, and by the end of the
second day Europe were ahead 9–7. The momentum swung Europe's
way in the second day fourball when Craig Stadler missed a three-foot
putt on the 18th to allow Langer and Sandy Lyle to halve the match.
With four wins and a half on the opening six singles – Masters champion
Langer claiming the penultimate point with a 5&4 win over Hal Sutton
– Europe needed only one more point to clinch the Cup, and it was all
down to Sam Torrance, playing against US Open champion Andy North.

North hit his drive into water at the 18th and Torrance smashed a
long drive to within a nine-iron shot from the green, then hit his next
to 18ft and sank the putt for a birdie. Europe had won the Ryder Cup
for the first time in 28 years, and by margin of five points. A tearful
Torrance celebrated with his team-mates on the green.

Result: Europe 16.5, USA 11.5

1987, MUIRFIELD VILLAGE, OHIO
CAPTAINS: TONY JACKLIN (EUROPE), JACK NICKLAUS (USA)
After PGA officials and the European team held a meeting to clear the
air, during which various contentious issues were resolved, Europe shot
into a 10.5–5.5 lead by the end of the second day. The Spanish duo Seve
Ballesteros and José Maria Olazábal won their three matches and the
Europeans claimed all four fourballs on the afternoon of the second day.

A crucial match on day three was between Eamonn Darcy and Ben
Crenshaw. Darcy was two ahead by the sixth hole and Crenshaw broke
his putter in disgust. The American then had to putt for the rest of the
match with a one-iron and the edge of his sand wedge. Darcy
unsurprisingly ended up winning the match on the 18th, rolling in a 5ft

par putt while Crenshaw could only bogey. Ballesteros secured victory by beating Curtis Strange 2&1 and Europe retained the Cup with their first-ever win on American soil.

Result: Europe 15, USA 13

1989, THE BELFRY, WEST MIDLANDS
CAPTAINS: RAY FLOYD (USA), TONY JACKLIN (EUROPE)
Passions ran high in the European camp after US captain Ray Floyd introduced his team at the gala ball as 'the 12 greatest players in the world'. Floyd's confidence was misplaced by the end of the second day, as Europe were 9–7 ahead. Ballesteros and Olazábal were again critical for Europe, winning two and halving the third of their matches, while in the singles Ronan Rafferty demonstrated the unpredictability of the tournament when he beat British Open champion Mark Calcavecchia by one hole. Christy O'Connor played the shot of his life when he hit a two-iron from 220 yards to within 4ft of the pin on the 18th, which enabled him to beat Fred Couples by one hole. This shot virtually ensured Europe's retention of the trophy, which was confirmed when Canizares won the next match. With four matches remaining in the singles, Europe were four ahead, but Mark McCumber, Tom Watson, Lanny Wadkins and Curtis Strange all won. For only the second time in the Cup's history, the match was halved.

Result: Europe 14, USA 14

1991, KIAWAH ISLAND, SOUTH CAROLINA
CAPTAINS: BERNARD GALLACHER (EUROPE), DAVE STOCKTON (USA)
In the aftermath of Operation Desert Storm, this confrontation was billed by the press as 'the War on the Shore'. Indeed, a mood of fierce patriotism was evident in the behaviour of the spectators and the determination of the US team.

By the end of the second day, the scores were 8–8. Ballesteros and Olazábal were again the anchor for the Europeans, with three wins and one half, including one bad-tempered match, amid accusations of cheating, against Paul Azinger and Chip Beck. In the singles, Mark Calcavecchia led Colin Montgomerie by four with four to play, but Calc collapsed to scramble a half.

The destination of the Cup was decided on the last green of the last match, where Bernhard Langer conceded Hale Irwin's bogey putt,

— A POTTED HISTORY OF THE RYDER CUP (CONT'D) —

putted for a birdie from 45ft, and rolled the ball past the cup by 6ft. He then missed the return putt, which effectively halved the match, giving victory to the USA. Ballesteros later judged, 'No one could have holed that putt.' The Ryder Cup was back in US hands.

Result: USA 14.5, Europe 13.5

1993, THE BELFRY, WEST MIDLANDS
CAPTAINS: BERNARD GALLACHER (EUROPE), TOM WATSON (USA)
Trailing by one hole at the end of the second day of the 30th Ryder Cup, the US team stormed the singles, winning six and halving two. Ray Floyd – at 51, the oldest competitor in Ryder Cup history – sank three birdie putts on the back nine to beat Olazábal by two holes; Chip Beck came back from three holes down to beat Barry Lane by one; rookie Davis Love III sank a par putt on the final hole to win by one hole against Costantino Rocca; and Tom Kite had a resounding 5&3 victory over Bernhard Langer. Again, while the US had shown their nervousness in fourball and foursomes, their supremacy in singles was undisputed, and they retained the Ryder Cup.

Result: USA 15, Europe 13

1995, OAK HILL, NEW YORK
CAPTAINS: BERNARD GALLACHER (EUROPE), LANNY WADKINS (USA)
This was another tense match, won at the dying stages and featuring two holes in one from Howard Clarke and Costantino Rocca.

By the end of the second day, the USA were two ahead. A 6&5 win by Sam Torrance and Rocca in the morning foursomes against Davis Love III and Jeff Maggert had injected confidence into the Europeans, but three US wins in the afternoon had given the USA the lead going into the third day. This time, however, it was Europe's turn to shine in the singles. Unusually, five games went to the final hole, with the Europeans winning 4.5 points. Montgomerie, Faldo and Torrance won three games in succession, and then Corey Pavin pulled one back for the US, beating Langer. If Philip Walton could then beat Jay Haas, the Cup was coming back to Europe.

Walton was three ahead with three remaining but lost the 16th and

17th. On the 18th, a putt for a bogey 5 was enough to halve the hole and win the match.

Result: Europe 14.5, USA 13.5

1997, VALDERRAMA, SOTOGRANDE, SPAIN
CAPTAINS: SEVE BALLESTEROS (EUROPE), TOM KITE (USA)

In the first Ryder Cup to be played in continental Europe, the home team featured five rookies – Thomas Bjorn, Darren Clarke, Ignacio Garrido, Jesper Parnevik and Lee Westwood – while the USA fielded Tiger Woods, Justin Leonard and Davis Love III, who were Masters, British Open and USPGA champions, respectively. Over the match, however, the champions could only manage 1.5 points between them, and Ballesteros was everywhere in his buggy, encouraging their European opponents.

By the end of the second day, Europe were a massive 10.5–5.5 points ahead, thanks partly to Langer and Montgomerie's 5&3 win over Woods and O'Meara and Olazábal and Rocca's 5&4 defeat of Love and Fred Couples. The singles began with Couples trouncing Ian Woosnam 8&7, but Rocca adjusted the balance with a 4&2 defeat of Woods, and when Langer beat Brad Faxon by one hole, the Cup was retained. Montgomerie made sure of outright victory when he conceded a 20ft putt to Scott Hoch on the 18th green to halve the game.

Result: Europe 14.5, USA 13.5

1999, THE COUNTRY CLUB, BROOKLINE, MASSACHUSSETS
CAPTAINS: BEN CRENSHAW (USA), MARK JAMES (EUROPE)

This was yet another exciting match which went virtually to the wire. UK Captain Mark James had decided to leave out three players – Jean Van de Velde, Jarmo Sandelin and Andrew Coltart – until the singles, a ploy that appeared to work as Europe sped to a 10–6 lead by the end of day two. In that match, however, the US were dominant, winning the first seven games. The three European debutants were defeated early on: Van de Velde 6&5 by Love, Sandelin 4&3 by Mickelson and Coltart 3&2 by Woods. Although Harrington and Lawrie both won, a half would give outright victory to the USA, and this was duly accomplished in the penultimate game. Leonard, having snatched back four holes from Olazábal with seven remaining, sank an amazing 50ft putt on the 17th to go one ahead, with Olazábal still

— A POTTED HISTORY OF THE RYDER CUP (CONT'D) —

to putt. The US team and supporters raced onto the green in celebration, angering the Europeans, whose Colin Montgomerie was still out on the course with Payne Stewart.

Result: USA 14.5, Europe 13.5

2002, THE BELFRY, WEST MIDLANDS
CAPTAINS: CURTIS STRANGE (USA), SAM TORRANCE (EUROPE)
Moved back one year because of the World Trade Center attack on 11 September 2001, this tournament was decided in the singles match.

On the final day, the US and Europe were both on eight points. Captain Torrance had decided to open with his seven best players, and Europe took 4.5 points from the first six games, including a Harrington 5&4 win over Calcavecchia and a Montgomerie 5&4 defeat of Hoch (Monty was unbeaten in all of his five games). Strange had left his two best players – Woods and Mickelson – until last, but they were too late to halt the European momentum. In the eighth game, Azinger holed a birdie bunker shot for a half on the 18th to keep the US in with a faint chance, but Philip Price sank a long putt at the 16th for a famous 3&2 defeat of Phil Mickelson.

Europe got the half they needed when Paul McGinley came back from being two down with six to play to sink a par putt from 9ft on the 18th for victory, and his delighted team-mates threw the Irishman into the lake beside the 18th green. A beaming Torrance commented, 'I led them to the water and they drank copiously.'

Result: Europe 15.5, USA 12.5

2004, OAKLAND HILLS, MICHIGAN
CAPTAINS: BERNHARD LANGER (EUROPE), HAL SUTTON (USA)
A triumph of teamwork and discipline by Langer and his men secured the Cup for Europe by the amazing margin of 18.5–9.5, helped by the US's inability to recover from adversity. Nor was Sutton's gameplan enhanced by Chris Riley stating that he was too tired to play in the afternoon foursomes on the second day.

The US reeled in the face of such an onslaught and were the losing side for the sixth time in ten matches. Behind on day one by 6.5 to 1.5, by the end of the second day they were still 11–5 down against the battling Europeans. US captain Hal Sutton's controversial plan of pairing Tiger Woods and Phil Mickelson backfired, and this was compounded by his decision to put out his best three players on the final day.

The Cup was retained by Lee Westwood's winning putt against Kenny Perry with seven matches still out on the course, and the trophy was won outright when Colin Montgomerie holed a 4ft putt on the 18th. As a proud Monty rightly claimed after the tournament, 'We hit more fairways than they did, we hit more greens in regulation, and so we holed more putts than they did.' The Europeans all flew home together, while the US players went their separate ways by private jets, a fitting comment on which team had more of the collective spirit.

Result: Europe 18.5, USA 9.5

— BEATLEMANIA —

At the time of writing (June 2005), the US media are proclaiming the emergence of a new Fab Four: Vijay Singh, Tiger Woods, Phil Mickelson and Ernie Els. Admittedly, these players are streets ahead of the nearest competition (although Retief Goosen could be Stuart Sutcliffe, the fifth Beatle), but how apt are the comparisons with The Beatles of the 1960s?

Tiger Woods would have to be John Lennon, with his smouldering, trigger-hair temperament and his articulate self-belief, bordering on arrogance. Cuddly Phil, meanwhile, is the Macca of the group, his well-groomed, childlike features, and even his left-handedness, suiting him perfectly for the role of the cute moptop. Vijay Singh is George Harrison, his obsession with practice and his preference for remaining in the background also the hallmark of the lead guitarist. The 'Big Easy', however, can be none other than Ringo, his amiable, grinning manner and liking for a few beers accurately reflecting the essence of the wacky drummer.

So what would be on the first album from Fab Four, Mk 2? Obviously we'd have to start with 'Tax Man' and 'Baby You're A Rich Man'. Then we'll have 'Carry That Weight' (dedicated to their caddies), 'Fixing A Hole' (dedicated to the groundsmen), 'Magical Mystery Tour' (dedicated to the USPGA), 'I Am The Walrus' (dedicated to Craig Stadler), 'All You Need Is Love' (dedicated to Davis Love), 'Being For The Benefit Of Mr Kite' (dedicated to Tom Kite), 'Norwegian Wood' (dedicated to Mr Ping), 'When I'm 64' (dedicated to that perfect round) and 'Hey Jude' (dedicated to the FedEx St Jude Classic). And who would be The Rolling Stones? Answers on a scorecard, please…

— ALLISS' HALL OF FAME: GENE SARAZEN —

Born Eugene Saraceni in upstate New York, Gene Sarazen was a podgy, 5ft 3in figure with a strong baseball grip, but he nonetheless became one of America's finest ever golfers.

Like many other top professionals, Sarazen started his career as a caddie, but by the time he'd reached the tender age of 21 he'd collected three Major victories. He won his first US Tour event, the New Orleans Open, in 1920, and his first Major, the US Open, in 1922, shooting a record final round of 68. While waiting for the favourites to finish, he commented, 'I've got mine. Let them get theirs.' Later in the year he won the USPGA, becoming the first player to win both Major titles in the same year, and then defeated his great rival Walter Hagen in a 72-hole unofficial 'world championship'. The following year he beat Hagen again in the USPGA to pick up his third Major.

In Sarazen's day, bunker shots were difficult, with professionals content simply to blast the ball out of the sand, and Sarazen's lasting contribution to the game was the invention of the sand wedge, which gives players the ability to slice through the sand and float the ball in the desired direction. His accurate playing and his deftness in the bunkers brought him a total of 38 PGA titles in his career.

Nine years after his last Major victory, he won the British Open at Sandwich by five strokes and, two weeks later, shot a record score of 66 in his final round of the US Open to win the tournament by three shots. The following year he became the first man in golfing history to claim all four Majors when, after having double-eagled the 15th at Augusta, he won in a playoff. He never won another Major, but he played on until the 1940s, after which he retired and engaged in various lucrative businesses, including writing and farming on his estate.

— MONTY MAKES IT SEVEN —

Since 1937, the European PGA has awarded the Harry Vardon Trophy to the player who each season leads the Order of Merit. Prior to 1971, when the European Tour was officially formed, only two players – Charlie Ward in 1948/9 and Christy O'Connor in 1961/2 – had won the trophy two years in succession. Peter Oosterhuis then won it for four consecutive years, from 1971 to 1974, and Seve Ballesteros made it a hat-trick from 1976 to 1978. Great golfers both,

Oosterhuis and Ballesteros were the leading players on Tour in the 1970s.

No one has ever dominated the trophy, however, to the extent of Colin Montgomerie, who turned the European Tour into his own personal fiefdom between 1993 and 1999, winning the Volvo-sponsored Order of Merit a staggering seven times in succession. The often irascible Scotsman with the elegantly grooved swing, long accurate drives and no-nonsense technique won no fewer than 20 official tournaments and made 58 other top-ten appearances during this period. On occasion a good example of PG Wodehouse's remark about it not being difficult to tell the difference between a Scotsman with a grievance and a ray of sunshine, Montgomerie nevertheless can also be articulate and charming and is a gracious ambassador for the Tour and European golf generally.

Monty announced his arrival on Tour when he won the Portuguese Open in 1989, then going on to win the Scandinavian Masters in 1991. He set off on his record-breaking run in 1993 with victories in the Heineken Dutch Open and Volvo Masters, and he concluded with five wins in 1999, including his first win on his native soil – the Standard Life Loch Lomond – and his second successive Volvo PGA Championship title to net an official Money List record of over £1.3 million.

Curiously, however, Monty has never won a Major. Although he was prematurely congratulated by Jack Nicklaus on his victory at the US Open at Pebble Beach in 1992, a battling Tom Kite overtook him at the last moment to clinch the title. He was narrowly defeated by Ernie Els in the same tournament in 1994 and 1997, and he lost out to Steve Elkington in a playoff at the 1995 USPGA.

Montgomerie's hegemony on the European Tour came to an end in 2000 when Lee Westwood won six events on Tour to claim the Order of Merit and set a new Money List record of over £1.8 million. Although Monty remains an inspirational figure in the Ryder Cup, he has won only six times on Tour in the five years since he ceded his title.

— YOUR HONOUR, MR PRESIDENT —

Since William McKinley first developed an interest in the game in the 1890s, there has been a long tradition of US presidents on the golf course, exhibiting varying degrees of skill. Indeed, only four presidents in the last century didn't play the game. So here, in chronological order, are the golfing presidents from the beginning of the 20th century:

- **William Howard Taft** (1909–13) – Despite his 300lb frame, Taft was capable of scoring in the high 80s, though his girth was such that his caddy had to tee the ball up for him. He always used the Schenectady Putter, a centre-shafted club banned from tournament play. On one occasion, he cancelled a meeting with the President of Chile, muttering, 'I'll be damned if I'll give up my game to see this fellow.' His predecessor, Theodore Roosevelt, tried to warn him off the game, considering it a 'sissy sport'.

- **Woodrow Wilson** (1913–21) – A late convert to the game, Wilson was a true enthusiast, playing up to six times a week, using a red ball in the snow. He once remarked, 'While you're playing, you can't be worried and preoccupied with affairs.' He was, however, spectacularly hopeless, often shooting 120.

- **Warren Harding (1921–3)** – An inveterate gambler, Harding bet his way around the course, with his butler bringing him a whisky and soda every few holes.

- **Calvin Coolidge (1923–9)** – Like Wilson, Coolidge was pretty useless on the golf course, although he didn't share Wilson's fanatical enthusiasm for golf.

- **Franklin D Roosevelt (1933–45)** – A talented golfer and long hitter, Roosevelt had to give up the game when he was struck by polio at the age of 39. However, he oversaw the construction of more than 250 golf courses during his presidency.

- **Dwight Eisenhower (1953–61)** – Another late convert to the game, Eisenhower had a putting green built on the White House lawn and played over 800 games during his presidency. He frequently played Augusta (once shooting 79) and asked that a tall pine on the 17th hole be cut down as his ball kept hitting it. The tree remains, however, and is now known as the 'Ike Tree'. Bob Hope once remarked of Ike's golfing prowess, 'If he slices the budget like he slices a ball, the nation has nothing to worry about.' With his friend Arnold Palmer, Eisenhower is credited with initiating the golf boom of the 1950s and 1960s.

- **John F Kennedy (1961–3)** – The best of the bunch was Kennedy, who played golf for Harvard Freshmen and could shoot in the 70s. He avoided being seen too much on the golf course because, as a man of the 'common people', he didn't want to be associated with a rich man's sport. He was no expert at manoeuvring a golf cart, though, once turning one over on a narrow bridge at Palm Beach Country Club and suffering a soaking in a pond. Years after his death, a set of his clubs was auctioned for $700,000.

- **Lyndon Johnson (1963–9)** – Another golfing duffer, Johnson once played against Eisenhower, who won the first 17 holes, while Johnson won the last. He used to whack his way round the course, rarely bothering to count his score.

- **Richard Nixon (1969–74)** – Good enough to beat Eisenhower in a one-off match, Nixon gave away golf balls bearing the presidential seal and his name as gifts, and after his resignation he commented, 'Golf became my lifesaver.' His VP, Spiro Agnew, was a menace on the golf course, hitting three spectators with his first two shots at the 1971 Bob Hope Desert Classic before giving up for the day.

— YOUR HONOUR, MR PRESIDENT (CONT'D) —

- **Gerald Ford (1974–7)** – A fine athlete in his youth, Ford was a decent golfer, shooting in the mid-80s, although he could be temperamental, once smashing his driver into a tee box after a particularly nasty slice. His driving was, at best, erratic, and spectators had to be careful. As Bob Hope quipped, 'Gerald Ford made golf a contact sport.'

- **Ronald Reagan (1981–9)** – At his best, Reagan played off around a 12 handicap. There is a famous 1985 photograph of him practising his putting on Air Force One.

- **George Bush (1989–93)** – Son of Prescott Bush, one-time President of the USGA, Bush could shoot in the 70s, and one of his tee shots at the 1993 Doug Sanders Celebrity Classic struck Vice-President Dan Quayle on the head. Bush played Bill Clinton and Gerald Ford in the first round of the Bob Hope Classic in 1995 and defeated Clinton by one shot and Ford by eight.

- **Bill Clinton (1993–2001)** – During his Arkansas youth, Clinton was a caddy, and he has broken 80, once playing Johnny Miller in a match where he posted 89 to the US and UK Open champion's 69. During his presidency, Clinton was well known for the number of mulligans and gimmes he took and was occasionally accused of 'an inability to count strokes'. He would stroll around the course, often taking at least five hours to complete a round.

- **George W Bush (2001–present)** – With a smooth swing, Bush has a handicap of 15, although he is let down by his short game. He likes to play 'speed golf', finishing a round in under two hours. During the 1999 Ryder Cup, when the US team were losing 10–6 after the second day, he read them the letter that Colonel William Barrett Travis wrote when surrounded by Mexican troops at the Alamo and ends with 'Victory or death'. They won the trophy.

— LONG HITTER —

In the 1992 Texas Open, at San Antonio's Oak Hills GC, journeyman professional Carl Hooper hooked a drive that ended up hitting a cart path and continuing on for 787 yards until being stopped by a fence. After returning to the fairway by hitting two four-irons and then an eight-iron, Hooper took a double-bogey six and missed the cut.

— CALL ME TIGER —

Most people have nicknames, so why should golfers be any different? Here's a brief selection of today's names and those from the past, in no particular order:

Ben Hogan ......'Bantam Ben' (due to his size, at 5ft 9in and 150lb); 'the Wee Ice Mon' (after his nerveless display in winning the British Open at Carnoustie in 1953)

Eldrick Woods......'Tiger' (after his Dad's buddy in the Vietnam War)

Bobby Jones................'Bonnie Bobby' (christened by the admiring crowds at St Andrews in 1927 when Jones won the British Open by six strokes)

Arnold Palmer ....'The King' (for obvious reasons)

Lee Trevino ....'Supermex' (due to his Mexican background and habit of winning golf tournaments)

Billy Caspar ....'Buffalo Billy' (he used to eat buffalo meat to keep his weight down)

Greg Norman................'The Great White Shark' (just look at him)

Tommy Armour.......'The Silver Scot' (he was known as 'The Black Scot' until he got older and his hair turned grey)

Ernie Els.........................'The Big Easy' (due to his size and languid appearance)

Jim Barnes ....'Long Jim' (all 6ft 3in of him)

Corey Pavin ....'Bulldog' (the little man never gives up)

Bobby Locke ....'Muffin' (due to the size of his jowls)

Henry Picard..................'The Chocolate Soldier' (he was pro at the Hershey Country Club, Pennsylvania)

Harry Cooper...............'Lighthorse' (coined by Damon Runyan for the speed at which Cooper played the game)

Ben Crenshaw ....'Gentle Ben' (because of his fierce temper)

Henry Cotton...............................'Concentration Henry' (coined by Walter Hagen for obvious reasons)

Frank Urban Zoeller ....'Fuzzy' (the initial letters of his name)

Fred Couples ....'Boom Boom' (for his distance off the tee)

— CALL ME TIGER (CONT'D) —

Craig Stadler ....'Walrus' (because of his bulky shape and bushy moustache)

Phil Mickelson ....'Lefty' (he plays golf left-handed but, oddly, does everything else right-handed)

Hal Sutton ....'Halimony' (the US 2004 Ryder Cup captain is on his fourth wife)

John Daly...........................'Wild Thing' (divorces, alcohol-induced tantrums, fights – you name it)

Isao Aoki ....'The Tower' (at over 6ft, he's big in Japan)

Tim Herron ....'Lumpy' (a reference to his girth)

Mike Reid......................'Radar' (he's an extremely accurate golfer)

Joanne Carner................'Big Momma' (again, for obvious reasons)

Craig Parry............................'Popeye' (he has enormous forearms)

Jack Nicklaus............... 'Ohio Fats' (a disparaging reference coined earlier in his career from 'Arnie's Army'); now 'the Golden Bear' (due to his aggressive play on the course and massive wealth off it)

Gene Sarazen......................'The Country Squire' (after his estate in northeast USA)

Sergio Garcia....................'El Niño' (his performance resembles the power of the raging Spanish wind)

Scott Hoch ....'Hoch the Choke' (an unkind reference to his habits in the Majors)

Mark James.........................'Jesse' James (not particularly original)

Gil Morgan...............................'Doc' (he is a qualified optometrist)

Eduardo Romero.............'El Gato' (Spanish for 'the Cat', from his ability to stalk opponents and win)

James Waldorf........................'Duffy' (he was known by his family as 'Little Duffer' when he was young)

Mildred Didrikson Zaharias ....'Babe' Zaharias (after Babe Ruth)

Tony Lema.....................'Champagne' Tony (a lifestyle description)

Paul Azinger.......................................'The Zinger' (again, obvious)

Davis Love III ....'Slick' (he is, in fact, anything but)

Billy Andrade...........................'Chachi' (due to his similarity to the
Happy Days character)

Steve Lowery ....'Yogi' (due to his similarity to the cartoon bear)

Gene Littler ....'Gene the Machine' (he has a perfect swing)

Michelle Wie ....'The Big Weasy' (after Ernie Els)

Mi-Hyun Kim/Hee Won Han/Se Ri Pak/Gloria Park .....'The Seoul
Sisters' (think South Korea)

Gary Player ....'Black Knight' (he plays in black)

KJ Choi ....'Tank' (he was a powerlifter in his youth)

Miguel Angel Jiminez ....'The Mechanic' (after his
consistency and love of cars)

Loren Roberts............'Boss of the Moss' (due to his putting ability)

Mi-Hyun Kim...'Peanut' (she's 5ft 1in tall)

Jesper Parnevik ....'Pink Panther' (because of his
colourful taste in clothes)

— THE SHOT HEARD AROUND THE WORLD —

To many US baseball fans, the 'shot heard around the world' was Bobby
Thomson's home run against the Dodgers in the 1951 National League playoff.
Before Thomson, however, was Gene Sarazen, competing in the 1935 Masters
at Augusta. On a cold, wet, final afternoon, Sarazen, playing with Walter
Hagen, teed off at the 15th hole – a 485-yard par five – and drove the ball
approximately 265 yards, leaving him 230 yards to reach the green. He knew
he needed to birdie three of the last four holes to tie with Craig Wood, who
had arrived at the clubhouse in the lead.

Sarazen looked over a small crest, down the long slope to the distant green,
protected by a pond at the front, took out his four-wood and launched the
ball on its way. It sailed over the pond, landed on the edge of the green, bounced
twice on the turf and rolled into the cup for a double-eagle (albatross),
accompanied by delighted screams from the gallery. He parred the remaining
three holes and defeated Wood in a 36-hole playoff the following day. That
shot and Sarazen's victory – which gave him the first professional Grand Slam
– put the Masters firmly on the world tournament map.

— US MONEY LIST, NOVEMBER 2004 —
(AFTER TOUR CHAMPIONSHIP)

1   Vijay Singh
2   Ernie Els
3   Phil Mickelson
4   Tiger Woods
5   Stewart Cink
6   Retief Goosen
7   Adam Scott
8   Stephen Ames
9   Sergio Garcia
10   Davis Love III
11   Todd Hamilton
12   Chris DiMarco
13   Stuart Appleby
14   Mike Weir
15   Mark Hensby
16   Rory Sabbatini
17   Jerry Kelly
18   Steve Flesch
19   Zach Johnson
20   Scott Verplank

— THE LEITH RULES —

- You must tee your ball within one club's length of the hole.
- Your tee must be on the ground.
- You are not to change the ball which you strike off the tee.
- You are not to remove stones, bones or any break club for the sake of playing your ball, except on the fair green, and that only within a club's length of your ball.

- If your ball comes among water, or any watery filth, you are at liberty to take out your ball and bringing it behind the hazard and teeing it, you may play it with any club and allow your adversary a stroke for so getting out your ball.

- If your balls be found anywhere touching one another, you are to lift the first ball 'til you play the last.

- At holeing you are to play your ball honestly for the hole, and not to play upon your adversary's ball, not lying in your way to the hole.

- If you should lose your ball by its being taken up, or any other way, you are to go back to the spot where you struck last and drop another ball and allow your adversary a stroke for the misfortune.

- No man at holeing his ball is to be allowed to mark his way to the hole with his club or anything else.

- If a ball be stopp'd by any person, horse or dog, or anything else, the ball so stopp'd must be played where it lyes.

- If you draw your club in order to strike and proceed so far in the stroke as to be bringing down your club; if then your club shall break in any way, it is to be accounted a stroke.

- He whose ball lyes farthest from the hole is obliged to play first.

- Neither trench, ditch nor dyke made for the preservation of the links, nor the Scholar's Holes or the soldier's lines, shall be accounted a hazard, but the ball is to be taken out, teed and play'd with any iron club.

— THE EARLY DAYS —

Golf was not, as it sometimes feels, invented by some malevolent spirit intent on instilling self-doubt, humility and, often, abject despair into the hearts of its millions of hacking adherents. Rather, like most sporting activities, it evolved over a long period of time.

There is evidence that some Egyptian pharaohs used wooden clubs to hit balls filled with clay and wool, and the ancient Romans had a game called *paganica* that involved using a club to propel a ball stuffed with feathers in the direction of an opponent's goal. As the Roman empire spread, similar pastimes emerged in the south of France *(jeu de mail)* and England *(cambuca)*. However, it was many centuries later, in

— THE EARLY DAYS (CONT'D) —

the Low Countries, that a recognisable progenitor of the modern game emerged.

In the early 14th century, the Dutch took advantage of their frozen canals by inventing a game whereby a stick was wedged into the ice and people wielding other sticks competed to hit it by clubbing a wooden ball. The game was also played indoors and a cross-country variant was established. Known as *het kolven* and played with a club called a *kolf*, it's plausible that the pastime spread to the east coast of Scotland via fisherman or traders and was adapted to the Scottish 'links' (the sandy, undulating and treeless area between the sea and the cultivated mainland). It's equally possible that the name of the modern game came from the Scottish verb *gowff* (to hit), but we'll probably never know the truth (although there are some who insist that it stands for Gentlemen Only, Ladies Forbidden).

What is undeniable is that, by the early 15th century, the Scots had added the diabolical dimension that defines the modern game: the hole. Originally a rabbit scrape marked by a seagull feather, the hole was the target for shepherds' crooks, with a stone acting as the ball. This basic game spread in popularity, so much so that in 1457 King James II of Scotland passed a decree banning it, as it interfered with necessary military activities, most notably archery; in the words of the decree, 'The futeball and the golfeby utterly cryit downe and not usit.' The following century, however, James IV of Scotland and Mary, Queen of Scots, became avid golfers. Indeed, the latter was sternly rebuked for playing the game only days after her husband, the foppish Lord Darnley, had been murdered. Mary was also responsible for introducing caddies to the game, the word deriving from the French *cadet*, meaning 'young French noblemen', whom Mary had taken over from her court in France.

Although always the people's game in Scotland, golf was hijacked by the wealthier classes, and the Gentlemen Golfers of Leith – now the Honourable Company of Edinburgh

Golfers – established the first golf club, Muirfield, in 1744, ten years before St Andrews' Royal and Ancient. These 'clubs' were not the clubs of today; rather, they were gatherings where drinking and eating took place and where the 'three-bottle man' (claret being the drink of choice) was esteemed. The St Andrews course originally had 22 holes, but in 1764 that was changed to 18, and over time this number gradually became the norm. Golf soon outgrew its native land, with the legendary R&A professional Old Tom Morris designing England's first course, at Westward Ho!, in 1864. In 1880, there were around 60 clubs in Great Britain; 30 years later, there were over 2,300.

By the end of the 19th century, golf had become an international sport, largely due to the enthusiastic efforts of Scottish travellers. Dunfermline golfer John Reid opened the first US course (three holes on a cow pasture in Yonkers, New York) in 1888 and later that year turned an adjacent 30-acre site into the US's first real course, naming it St Andrew's (ie with an apostrophe to distinguish it from the Scotland course). Shortly thereafter, Brookline Country Club (venue for the 1999 Ryder Cup) and Shinnecock Hills (a US Open regular) were established.

The Scottish crusading influence was also evident in the formation of India's Royal Calcutta Club – the world's oldest club outside the British Isles – in 1829; France's Pau, in 1856; New Zealand's Royal Christchurch, in 1867; Australia's Royal Adelaide, in 1870; and South Africa's Royal Cape, in 1885. And so the game spread over the globe.

— THE GREAT LEADER —

North Korean leader Kim Jong-Il is, according to the Pyongyang media, 'the world's greatest golfer'. Apparently in 1994, during the Great Leader's first attempt at golf, he started with an eagle two at the Pyongyang Golf Club and collected five holes in one on his way to carding a 38-under-par 34 over the 18 holes. Keep away from the North Korean Tour, Tiger.

— Q SCHOOL —

The USPGA Tour is a lucrative circuit. In the 2004 season, the top 77 players on the Money List grossed over £1 million each, with the leader, Vijay Singh, earning just under £11 million – and this is, of course, before their various endorsements and sponsorships kick in. That year, even the player in the 125th spot on the List earned just over $620,000.

In actual fact, the 125th spot is an important one. At the end of each season, the top 125 players on the Tour retain their card and playing privileges for the following season. There are also 34 'exemption categories', giving exemptions from qualifying in such areas as winners of Majors and various tournaments, past champions, medical and sponsors' exemptions, etc. Generally, however, if a professional finishes in 126th place or below, he faces a course at the Tour National Qualifying School. Known universally as 'Q School', these qualifying rounds take place between October and early December. Regarded as one of the most gruelling and agonising ordeals in golf, Q School is not for the faint-hearted.

There are three stages. The first two qualifying rounds are each of four rounds and the final round, with a field of 170, is over 108 holes at La Quinta, in California. Entrants have to pay $4,500 and satisfy various criteria of competence before they can participate, and there are again exemptions – for example, the players ranked from 126 to 150 in the previous year can go straight to the final qualifying round. The top 30-plus ties in the final round qualify to play on the following year's Tour, which, given that there are 1,200 applicants, means that only 2.5 per cent of those who enter can get through.

The pressures on the players at Q School are horrendous, given the vast awards that await them should they qualify. The field is made up mainly of college kids with a smattering of older players, ex-Tour professionals and professionals from other Tours, such as the European and Asian. Some make it, but of course there are many casualties:

- In 1995, Eric Epperson was near the lead with nine holes to play, then bogeyed six of the last nine and was out of contention.

- In 1999, Jaxon Brigman won his card by one shot but mistakenly signed for a 66 instead of the 65 he had scored. His signed score stood and he failed to get through.

- In 2001, Roland Thatcher was tied 35th – a score that at that time made him eligible for the Tour – on the last hole. His approach shot hit the clubhouse roof, costing him three strokes. No Tour for Roland.

- Also in 2001, Bud Still, playing the penultimate hole and in 35th position, stepped on his ball in a bunker, incurring a penalty shot. He missed his Tour card by one stroke.

- In 2000, Joe Daley stroked in a four-foot putt on the final hole and his ball came straight back out of the hole. He, too, failed to qualify by one stroke.

- In 2004, Isabelle Beisiegel, the first woman ever to attempt qualification through Q School, finished in last place in the first qualifying round.

But of course, there are also many success stories:

- In 1999, Gary Nicklaus qualified for the Tour on his ninth attempt, tieing for 12th position at Q School.

- Between 1998 and 2000, Cameron Beckman qualified for the Tour through Q School a record three times in succession.

- In 2001, Garrett Willis, who had qualified for the Tour the previous year through Q School, won the US Tucson Open, the first full-field event on Tour, and collected over $500,000. 'Ain't this a great country?' said Willis.

- Todd Hamilton, who qualified tied for 16th place in 2003 – his eighth attempt at Q School – won the British Open in his first year and earned over $3 million in 2004.

The competitors who finish between 31st and 80th place have the additional incentive of earning playing privileges on the Nationwide Tour. However, the leader in the 2004 Nationwide Money List, Jimmy Walker, earned just over $370,000 – the same as the player ranked 159th on the PGA Tour – so it's easy to understand the appeal of Q School.

— PLAYERS SPEAK OUT —

'This is a game of misses. The guy who misses the best is going to win.'
– Ben Hogan

'I'm glad I brought this course, this monster, to its knees.'
– Ben Hogan after his US Open victory at Oakland Hills in 1951

'He's got a swing like an octopus falling out of a tree.'
– David Feherty on Jim Furyk

'You don't know the meaning of pressure until you play for five bucks with two bucks in your pocket.'

– Lee Trevino

'All men are created equal. I'm just one stroke better than the rest.'
– Gene Sarazen on winning the 1922 US Open

'Arnold [Palmer] would never protect a lead. He'd go for the flag off an alligator's back.'

– Lee Trevino

'I could take out of my life everything except my experiences at St Andrews and I'd still have a rich, full life.'
– Bobby Jones on being awarded Freeman of St Andrews in 1958

'It doesn't hurt much anymore. These days I can go a full five minutes without thinking about it.'
– Doug Sanders reflecting on the 2ft putt he missed that would have won him the 1970 British Open at St Andrews 30 years earlier, when he was beaten by Jack Nicklaus in the playoff

'Every good man is tested in the crucible of humiliation.'
– Chip Beck after his 9&8 defeat by Seve Ballesteros in the 1989 World Matchplay Championship

'This speech is like my tee shot: I don't know where it's going.'
– José Maria Olazábal at a PGA European Tour dinner

'He's raised the bar to a level only he can reach.'
– Tom Watson on Tiger Woods after Woods' British Open win at St Andrews in 2000

'Competitive golf is played mainly on a five-and-a-half-inch course, the space between your ears.'

– Bobby Jones

'I'll always remember the day I broke 90. I had a few beers in the clubhouse and was so excited I forgot to play the back nine.'

– Bruce Lansky

'I'd like to see the fairways more narrow. Then everybody would have to play from the rough, not just me.'

– Seve Ballesteros

'When I'm on a golf course and it starts to rain and lightning, I hold up my one-iron, 'cause I know even God can't hit a one iron.'

– Lee Trevino

'Why waste good shots in practice when you might need them in a match?'

– Walter Hagen

— ALLISS' HALL OF FAME: JACK NICKLAUS —

Jack Nicklaus is arguably the greatest golfer ever to play the game. With a probably unbeatable record of 18 Majors and winner of 71 US Tour events, the 'Golden Bear' stands at the pinnacle of 20th-century golf.

The twice US Amateur champion from Columbus, Ohio, first came to national attention as a fresh-faced, chubby kid in the 1960 US Open, where he finished second to Arnold Palmer. He gained his revenge two years later, however, when he beat Palmer in a playoff at the same tournament in 1962. By 1963, after Nicklaus had won the USPGA and the Masters, Bobby Jones was remarking, 'He plays a game with which I am not familiar.' A slimmed-down Nicklaus, provoked into losing 3st by a spectator holding a sign reading PUT IT HERE, FAT BOY, had begun to take over Palmer's mantle.

Nicklaus's great rival then became Lee Trevino, who defeated him in a playoff at the 1970 US Open and in the 1972 British Open. The next opponent was Tom Watson, who defeated Nicklaus in a classic 1977 confrontation at the British Open

— ALLISS' HALL OF FAME: JACK NICKLAUS (CONT'D) —

at Turnberry and then again at the final hole of the US Open at Pebble Beach, denying Nicklaus a record fifth US Open title.

Altogether, Nicklaus played in six Ryder Cup teams (1969, 1971, 1973, 1975, 1977 and 1981), won four US Opens (1962, 1967, 1972 and 1980), three British Opens (1966, 1970 and 1978), five USPGAs (1963, 1971, 1973, 1975 and 1980) and six Masters (1963, 1965, 1966, 1972, 1975 and 1986). His final Masters win was the most remarkable, coming on the heels of a newspaper report the day before the tournament announcing that 'Nicklaus is all washed up.' Determined to disprove this, the 46-year-old Nicklaus, with his son Jackie caddying, shot a final-round 65 – including a barely believable six-under-par 30 on the back nine – to defeat Tom Kite and Greg Norman by one stroke.

Nicklaus joined the US Seniors' Tour in 1990 and has played a limited schedule of events but collected several million dollars in the process. His Golden Bear business conglomerate has many profitable interests, including equipment manufacture, publishing and golfing academies. He has also designed world-class golf courses, such as those at Muirfield Village in Ohio and Grand Cypress in Florida. The boy from Columbus has certainly travelled a long way in his 40 years in golf.

— GETTING BETTER WITH AGE —

Described as the world's most successful new sporting venture of the 1980s and 1990s, the US Seniors' Tour had modest beginnings. Formed after a meeting in January 1980 between Sam Snead, Gardner Dickinson, Bob Goalby, Don January, Don Sikes and Julius Boros, the new Tour – for professional golfers aged 50 plus – held two tournaments in its first year, with total prize money of £250,000. By 1984, the Tour had expanded to 24 tournaments and was handing out $5 million in prize money.

The involvement of Arnold Palmer from the outset was critical to the Tour's success, and the arrival of Gary Player and Peter Thomson in

1985, followed by Jack Nicklaus in 1990, made the Tour an even more lucrative attraction for the USPGA and the ageing players. The audience demographic – normally the same age as the players and wealthy business people – brought advertising and sponsorship flooding in to the Tour, and the pro-am match that accompanies each tournament gives them the opportunity to play with their heroes.

It wasn't only the big names who prospered, however: Jim Dent – winless in his 18-year career on the PGA Tour – joined the Seniors in 1989 and has won 12 Senior events to date, amassing over $9 million; Jim Albus, who never played on the PGA Tour and came straight to the Seniors from his job as a Long Island golf pro, claimed six events between 1991 and 1998 and earned over $6 million; and Allen Doyle, who played most of his career as an amateur, joined the Senior Tour in 1998 and has won nine tournaments to date, collecting more than $10 million in winnings.

The number of participants on the US Senior Tour is normally 78, comprising the top 32 all-time earners, the top 31 from the previous season, the top eight from Qualifying School and four sponsors' invitees, while the remaining places are taken by the successful contenders in the qualifying event on the Monday before the tournament. The events on the Tour are usually held over 54 holes between Friday and Sunday, with the exception of the four Majors, which are 72 holes and last for four days each. In 2004, 30 official events were held on what is now known as the Champions Tour for total prize money of $52 million.

The leading money-earner in the history of the Tour is Hale Irwin, who, in addition to his three US Open and 17 other USPGA titles, has notched up 40 tournament successes with the Seniors and earned a staggering $26.5 million. Gil Morgan, who enjoyed a steady if unspectacular career on the regular Tour, and US Open winner Tom Kite are next in the listings, earning just under $20 million apiece.

The emergence of Tiger Woods and the renewed interest in the main Tour has in recent years seen the spotlight move away from the Seniors' event. To counter this, discussions have been taking place about lowering the minimum age for entry to 45 and even introducing a Seniors' Ryder Cup. The Champions Tour, however, with its regular intake of household names, will remain a vibrant part of the US golfing scene.

— THE PERFECT SWING —

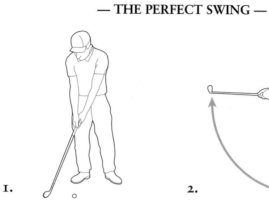

1.

2.

3.

4.

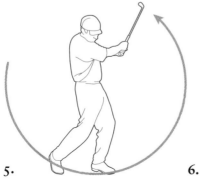

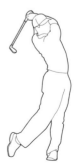

5.

6.

— THE TIGER SLAM —

By winning the 2001 Masters, Tiger Woods became the first golfer in history to be reigning champion of all four Major tournaments simultaneously. He began this extraordinary, unprecedented run of victories at the 2000 US Open at Pebble Beach, where he shot a record-equalling, 12-under-par 272 to finish 15 strokes ahead of Ernie Els and Miguel Angel Jiminez, the biggest winning margin in the history of any of the Major tournaments. His opening round of 65 was the lowest opening round in the history of the US Open at Pebble Beach, he one-putted on no fewer than 34 holes and he didn't have a single three-putt. This win made Woods the all-time money-winner on the USPGA Tour.

In July 2000, at the Old Course, St Andrews, Woods shot four rounds in the 60s to record a 19-under-par 269, ending the event eight strokes ahead of Ernie Els (again) and Thomas Bjorn. His score – a record for the British Open at St Andrews – included 22 birdies. Despite there being 128 bunkers on the Old Course, he didn't visit any during his four rounds.

Woods was more fortunate to win the USPGA Championship the following month, his second straight victory in the event. He initially tied with journeyman Bob May on a record 18-under-par 270 at the Valhalla course at Louisville, Kentucky, and won the playoff over the final three holes by one shot, thus equalling Ben Hogan's record of three Majors in one season

In April 2001, Woods finished the Masters two shots ahead of David Duval and three in front of Phil Mickelson to claim his second Masters title and set his amazing record.

Although generally agreed not to represent a Grand Slam, as the tournaments didn't all take place in the same calendar year, it was allotted its own category as the 'Tiger Slam'. It seems extremely unlikely that such a record will ever be equalled – unless it's by the man himself.

— RULES OF GOLF —

Success in and enjoyment of golf depend crucially on individual honesty and integrity. Unlike most other sports, much of golf is not played in full view of one's opponents or a referee, and the opportunity for cheating – improving one's lie in the rough, for instance, or subtracting a shot or two from a round – is evident. Cheating in golf, however, is anathema to the average golfer, an affront to the essence of the game. As the great Bobby Jones remarked after calling on himself a penalty stroke for an infringement that nobody but he saw, 'You might as well praise me for not breaking into a bank. There is only one way to play this game.' And the 'only one way' is through strict adherence to the Rules of Golf.

The Rules of Golf are set, monitored and updated on a four-yearly basis by the Royal and Ancient and the USGA. The first rules were set by The Honourable Company of Edinburgh Golfers in 1744, but the basis for today's Rules were laid out by St Andrews in 1754. This blueprint contained 13 rules, the essence of which governed that players should 'play the ball as it lies', except for when it touched another ball or was unplayable in 'water or watery filth'. The ball could be lifted out of water at the expense of a stroke and a lost ball also cost a stroke, while obstructions, such as stones, could not be removed unless such objects were on the putting surface. The Rules became more complex with the increasing popularity of strokeplay (the original rules were for matchplay) and the need, for example, of a clearer definition of what is 'unplayable'.

In 1951, the R&A and USGA got together and established a clear codification of regulations for golf worldwide. Today there are 34 Rules, divided into a complex, almost labyrinthine array of subheadings, amendments and appendices covering everything from 'Player's Responsibilities' to 'Relief Situations', 'Procedure' and highly technical data on clubs and balls. The Rules aren't exactly light reading – and, in many cases, seem designed to confuse – but they are at the heart of the game. They are, of course, continually infringed, although in the majority of cases this is by accident rather than design, and top golfers are no more immune to the former than lowly hackers; Nick Faldo, for instance, was penalised on two consecutive days at the 1994 British Open for hitting the wrong ball, and Seve Ballesteros has said, 'There is a difference between cheating and breaking the rules.'

Newcomers to the game who find the Rules bewildering would do well to consider Tom Watson's view: 'There are only two basic rules that matter. One: play the ball as it lies. Two: if you don't know what to do next, do what you think is fair' – a reasonable maxim for most situations on the golf course. And, if you find yourself in a water hazard facing an immovable obstruction, don't even contemplate trying to understand Rule 24.2 Just ask someone...

— MILESTONES: A BRITISH OPEN TIMELINE —

The British Open is regarded as being the leading tournament in world golf. By some degree the oldest of the Majors, it also has a proud tradition that began – like everything else in the game – in Scotland.

When Allan Robertson – one of the age's outstanding professionals and a club and ball maker of repute – died in 1859, Major OJ Fairlie of Prestwick Golf Club suggested staging a professional tournament to decide who was the leading golfer in his place. Invitations for a competition were duly sent to St Andrews, Musselburgh, Bruntsfield, Leven, Carnoustie, Panmure, Montrose, Perth, Blackheath, Darlington Castle, North Berwick and Aberdeen, and the match would be contested over 36 holes in one day at Prestwick's 12-hole course.

Held under the auspices of Prestwick Golf Club, the first British Open – contested between eight professional golfers – took place on 17 October 1860. The first prize – a red morocco-leather Challenge Belt – was won by Willie Park Senior, who beat Old Tom Morris by two strokes.

The timeline below lists the major developments in the British Open's long life:

1861 The British Open is now open to the whole world, including amateurs. Old Tom wins this year's tournament.

— MILESTONES: A BRITISH OPEN TIMELINE (CONT'D) —

1862   Old Tom wins again by 13 strokes – a record-winning margin to this day.

1867   Old Tom wins his fourth and last title at the age of 46 years and 99 days. Today, he is still the oldest ever winner in the British Open's history.

1868   The dynasty continues, with Young Tom Morris claiming victory. At 17 years and 161 days, he is the youngest-ever winner of the British Open.

1872   Young Tom wins again, for the fourth and final time. His is the first name to be inscribed on the new trophy: a silver claret jug. Young Tom dies three years later, heartbroken by the death of his young wife.

1873   The British Open leaves Prestwick for the first time. Tom Kidd wins the first prize of £11 at St Andrews.

1890   John Ball becomes the first amateur and, indeed, the first Englishman to claim the British Open title.

1892   The tournament is held at Muirfield for the first time. Prize money is raised from £28 and 10 shillings to £110 to attract competitors from another competition at Musselburgh. An entry fee of 10 shillings is charged, and the British Open is now held over two days, with 72 holes. Another amateur, Harold Hilton, wins.

1894   The British Open is held outside Scotland for the first time, at Sandwich. JH Taylor wins, and the triumvirate of Taylor, Braid and Vardon begins its 16-year ascendancy in the event.

1898   Due to the high volume of entries, a cut is introduced after 36 holes at Prestwick. Willie Park Junior misses a 3ft putt at the last hole to hand victory to Vardon.

1902   Sandy Herd wins at Hoylake using the new, rubber-cored ball.

1904   Jack White collects the claret jug at Sandwich after becoming the first player to win with a score of under 300 (296).

1907   Qualifying rounds are introduced, with no exemptions. Frenchman Arnaud Massey becomes the first overseas British Open champion.

1920 The Open is held at Deal for the second and last time. The R&A take over responsibility for the championship.

1922 The R&A decree that only links courses will henceforth be used for the British Open. Walter Hagen becomes the first US winner at Royal St George's.

1923 Troon hosts the tournament for the first time.

1925 Prestwick hosts its 24th and final British Open.

1926 Bobby Jones becomes the second winner of the US Open, hitting a magnificent 180-yard shot from the fairway bunker at the penultimate hole to within 12ft of the pin. A plaque is erected on the 17th green to mark this shot.

1934 Henry Cotton wins the tournament, shooting a record-breaking 65 in his second round, to be the tournament's first British victor after ten successive US victories. The Dunlop 65 golf ball is manufactured to commemorate this feat.

1946 Crowd-control measures are introduced at St Andrews. 'Slammin' Sam' Snead wins the tournament.

1947 Fred Daly at Hoylake becomes the only Irishman to win the Open.

1951 Max Faulkner wins the only British Open ever to be played in Northern Ireland, at Portrush.

1960 At the centenary British Open at St Andrews, Arnold Palmer makes his first appearance, finishing second to Kel Nagle.

1963 New Zealander Bob Charles becomes the only left-handed player to lift the trophy.

1966 The tournament is extended from three to four days. Jack Nicklaus wins at Muirfield in first tournament broadcast in the USA, by ABC.

1974 With his third victory, at Royal Lytham, Gary Player becomes one of only three golfers to win in three separate decades.

1984 Seve Ballesteros prevents Tom Watson from claiming a record-equalling

— MILESTONES: A BRITISH OPEN TIMELINE (CONT'D) —

six British Open titles. Watson's second shot at the 17th lands beside a wall and Ballesteros birdies the hole at St Andrews.

1985 The four-hole playoff is introduced. Sandy Lyle beats Payne Stewart by one shot at Royal St George's.

1986 Greg Norman wins at Turnberry, posting a lowest-ever score of 63 in his second round.

1989 At Troon, Mark Calcavecchia wins the first ever three-way, four-hole playoff.

1990 A new record attendance for the tournament – over 208,000 – is set at St Andrews, where Faldo shoots 270 to win by five strokes.

1993 Greg Norman storms around Royal St George's, shooting a final-round 64 for a final score of 267, the lowest 72-hole total ever recorded in the British Open.

2000 In the 26th British Open at St Andrews, Tiger Woods shoots a 269 – at 19 under par, a new record for the Open – to destroy the field by eight strokes.

2001 David Duval banishes his Majors demons, winning the title by three strokes.

— ALLISS' HALL OF FAME: LEE TREVINO —

From humble beginnings in Texas, born to Mexican parents and growing up in a house without electricity or running water, the ebullient Lee Trevino rose to claim 27 US Tour events in total, along with three Open championships in the space of one month.

Learning his golf on a local municipal course, young Trevino joined the US Marines, taking a job as a club professional after his tour of duty. He entered his first US Tour event – the Texas State Open – in 1965, and in 1967 he finished fifth in the US Open to become Rookie of the Year. In the following year he stunned US golf by beating Jack Nicklaus by four shots in the US Open, in the process becoming the first ever player to shoot four below-par rounds in the tournament.

In 1971, Trevino was voted *Sports Illustrated* Sportsman of the Year for his remarkable achievements that season. That year, he first won the US Open for a second time, defeating Nicklaus again after an 18-hole playoff, then won the Canadian Open before travelling to Birkdale to defeat Lu Liang Huan by one shot to win the British Open. He returned to Muirfield the following year to defend his title, and his short-game prowess (and good fortune around the greens) helped him to beat Tony Jacklin and retain the trophy.

'Supermex', as he became known, is a colourful, larger-than-life personality who wisecracked his way around the course while remaining fully aware of the serious nature of his efforts. He played in six Ryder Cups and was captain of the 1985 squad that was defeated by Europe at the Belfry. He won his last Major – the USPGA – in 1984 at the age of 44, and six years later he joined the US Senior Tour, saying, 'No way I'm going to play with flatbellies when I can play with roundbellies.' To date, he has won over £13 million in this most lucrative of finales to a top golfer's career.

— US OPEN WINNERS —

2004	Retief Goosen
2003	Jim Furyk
2002	Tiger Woods
2001	Retief Goosen
2000	Tiger Woods
1999	Payne Stewart
1998	Lee Janzen
1997	Ernie Els
1996	Steve Jones
1995	Corey Pavin

— US OPEN WINNERS (CONT'D) —

1994...Ernie Els

1993...Lee Janzen

1992 ....Tom Kite

1991 ....Payne Stewart

1990...Hale Irwin

1989 ....Curtis Strange

1988 ....Curtis Strange

1987 ....Scott Simpson

1986 ....Ray Floyd

1985 ....Andy North

1984 ....Fuzzy Zoeller

1983...Larry Nelson

1982...Tom Watson

1981 ....David Graham

1980...Jack Nicklaus

1979...Hale Irwin

1978 ....Andy North

1977...Hubert Green

1976 ....Jerry Pate

1975 ....Lou Graham

1974...Hale Irwin

1973...Johnny Miller

1972...Jack Nicklaus

1971 ....Lee Trevino

1970...Tony Jacklin

1969 ....Orville Moody

1968 ....Lee Trevino

1967...Jack Nicklaus

1966 ....Billy Casper

1965 ....Gary Player

1964 ....Ken Venturi

1963 ....Julius Boros

1962 ....Jack Nicklaus

1961 ....Gene Littler

1960 ....Arnold Palmer

1959 ....Billy Casper

1958 ....Tommy Bolt

1957 ....Dick Mayer

1956 ....Cary Middlecoff

1955 ....Jack Fleck

1954 ....Ed Furgol

1953 ....Ben Hogan

1952 ....Julius Boros

1951 ....Ben Hogan

1950 ....Ben Hogan

1949 ....Cary Middlecoff

1948 ....Ben Hogan

1947 ....Lew Worsham

1946 ....Lloyd Mangrum

1942–45 ....Not played
due to World War II

1941 ....Craig Wood

1940 ....Lawson Little

1939 ....Byron Nelson

1938 ....Ralph Guldahl

1937 ....Ralph Guldahl

1936 ....Tony Manero

1935 ....Sam Parks Jr

— US OPEN WINNERS (CONT'D) —

1934 ....Olin Dutra

1933 ....Johnny Goodman

1932 ....Gene Sarazen

1931 ....Billy Burke

1930 ....Bobby Jones

1929 ....Bobby Jones

1928 ....Johnny Farrell

1927 ....Tommy Armour

1926 ....Bobby Jones

1925 ....W MacFarlane

1924...Cyril Walker

1923 ....Bobby Jones

1922 ....Gene Sarazen

1921...Jim Barnes

1920...Ted Ray

1919.....................................Walter Hagen

1917–18 ....Not played
due to World War I

1916...................................Charles Evans Jr

1915...................................Jerome Travers

1914.....................................Walter Hagen

1913 ....Francis Ouimet

1912 ....John McDermott

1911 ....John McDermott

1910 ....Alex Smith

1909...................................George Sargent

1908 ....Fred McLeod

1907...Alex Ross

1906 ....Alex Smith

1905	Willie Anderson
1904	Willie Anderson
1903	Willie Anderson
1902	Laurie Auchterlonie
1901	Willie Anderson
1900	Harry Vardon
1899	Willie Smith
1898	Fred Herd
1897	Joe Lloyd
1896	James Foulis
1895	Horace Rawlins

— THE GREAT TRIUMVIRATE —

Great golfers seem to come in threes. Think Hagen, Jones and Sarazen in the 1920s and 1930s; Hogan, Snead and Nelson in the 1940s; and Player, Palmer and Nicklaus in the 1960s. However, the first outstanding threesome, comprising Taylor, Braid and Vardon, was the most dominant of them all.

JH Taylor, James Braid and Harry Vardon between them won the British Open 16 times between 1894 and 1914 and ruled the world of golf for 20 years. Devon-born Taylor, who was expert at keeping the ball long and low (an advantage on windy courses), won the tournament in 1894 at St George's (the first British Open to be held outside Scotland) and in 1895 at St Andrews. In 1913 he won his fifth title and also achieved four second-place finishes in the tournament. He was an exponent of the 'mashie' (five-iron), which allowed him great accuracy in the wind.

Braid, the son of a ploughman from Fife, was an even longer hitter than Taylor and an accurate putter who won his first British Open in 1901 and his fifth in 1910 at St Andrews, making him the first man to win five British Opens. During the first decade of the 20th century, Braid established himself as the best player in the world.

Vardon, from the Channel Island of Jersey, gave his name to the 'Vardon grip', where the index finger of the left hand is overlapped by the little finger of the right, which he popularised, although it had

— THE GREAT TRIUMVIRATE (CONT'D) —

been in use for some years. In contrast to Taylor, Vardon developed
a graceful swing that allowed him to hit the ball high and thereby
hold the fairways and greens, and his accuracy off the tee was
legendary. He beat Taylor in a 36-hole playoff at the 1896 British
Open and won his third Open in 1899 before going to America and
winning the US Open the following year, with Taylor in second place.
In 1914 he won his sixth British Open and remains the only man to
have claimed the Claret Jug on six occasions.

These legendary golfers played in a period when British golf was
dominant. As their careers came to an end, however, the balance of
power was swinging to America. Johnny McDermott became the first
home-grown winner of the US Open in 1911, and two years later
American amateur Francis Ouimet's victory in a playoff with Vardon
and fellow Englishman Ted Ray marked the beginning of the of the
end of the Triumvirate and an explosion of interest in golf in the USA.

— ALLISS' HALL OF FAME: NICK FALDO —

A single-minded, dedicated personality, Nick Faldo became
the most successful British player of his generation, and
arguably the best English golfer since Harry Vardon. Noted
for his mental strength and determination, he is one of the
best mid-iron players in the game and is renowned for his
straightness off the tee.

A comparative latecomer to golf (he started at the age of 13
after watching Jack Nicklaus on TV), Faldo won the English
Youth Amateur title at the age of 18 and his first European
Tour event two years later in 1977, the same year that he
defeated Masters and British Open champion Tom Watson
in the Ryder Cup at Royal Lytham. He won the European
Order of Merit in 1983 and his first USPGA Tour tournament
– the Sea Pines Heritage Classic – in 1984. However,
concerned about the reliability of his swing and its inability
to stand up to the pressures of Major tournaments, he linked
up with coach David Ledbetter in the mid-1980s, remodelled
his swing and his career took off. His first Major win came
in 1987 at the British Open at Muirfield, a tournament at
which he was one stroke behind leader Paul Azinger by the

beginning of the final round but went on to par every remaining hole to lift the trophy.

Success in the USA arrived two years later at the Masters. Although poor putting contributed to a 77 in his third round, Faldo shot a magnificent 65 in the last round to tie for a playoff with Scott Hoch, whom he defeated on the second extra hole. Accompanied by caddie Fanny Sunneson, he won again at Augusta in 1990, beating Ray Floyd in another playoff, and became the first player to win two successive Masters titles since Jack Nicklaus in 1965/6. In the same year he also lifted the British Open claret jug with an emphatic five-shot win over Mark McNulty and Payne Stewart, while at the 1992 British Open at Muirfield he claimed his fifth Major, birdying two of the last four holes to overtake John Cook in a dramatic finale to the championship.

Faldo's Ryder Cup record is outstanding, the British golfer having played in 11 competitions and holding the record number of points (25). His finest moment was in 1995, when he recovered from being one down with two to play against Curtis Strange to beat the American and help lead Europe to victory.

Faldo's final victory in the Majors came in 1996, when Greg Norman threw away a six-shot lead over the Englishman at the start of the final round to collapse in the face of Faldo's relentless onslaught over the Augusta fairways. Since then, Faldo has won no tournaments, but, although age is no longer on his side, few would bet against this most intensely competitive of players collecting another trophy.

— FATALITIES —

Ed Harrison was playing by himself at Inglewood Country Club in Seattle. As he teed off, the shaft of his driver broke and pierced his groin. He collapsed with shock and bled to death.

In Montreal, Rudolph Ray was killed when, playing out of trees, his club shaft broke and rebounded off a tree, the jagged edge penetrating his body and killing him.

— THE GREAT BATTLES OF GOLF HISTORY 3 —

TOM WATSON V JACK NICKLAUS, BRITISH OPEN, TURNBERRY, 1977

Generally regarded as one of the finest four rounds of golf ever played, this was an epic battle between two of the titans of the modern game. Fought at a sun-drenched Turnberry – the first time this west-of-Scotland course had staged the British Open – by the end of the third round Watson and Nicklaus were so far ahead of the rest of the field that they were virtually uncatchable. After three masterclasses of faultless strokemaking, the duo were both on 203 and their scorecards were identical: 68–70–65.

On the final round, Nicklaus commanded the early stages and was one shot ahead at the turn. A long putt gave him a two-stroke lead on the 12th, but then Watson birdied the 13th to go one under. As they stood on the 14th tee, Watson turned to Nicklaus and said, 'This is what it's all about, isn't it, Jack?' Nicklaus nodded assent. Watson then went level with another birdie on the 15th. Two holes later, Nicklaus mishit a four-iron on the 17th and Watson birdied, taking the slender American one stroke ahead.

By the final hole of the tournament, the destination of the Claret Jug had still not been decided. Watson hit a straight one-iron off the tee while Nicklaus's driver found some gorse. Watson's second shot landed just a few feet from the pin while Nicklaus slashed out off the bushes to land some 30ft from the flag. Nicklaus, incredibly, putted out for a birdie, but Watson held his nerve to do the same and become British Open champion, for the second time, by one shot, leaving the third-placed player, Hubert Green, a distant 11 shots behind.

Watson would win three further British Opens, but none matched the unbelievable tension of this contest or the single-minded determination and technical quality of the Kansas City man's victory against a player who's commonly held to be the best golfer in the world.

— HUBRIS...AND NEMESIS —

US pro Grier Jones was playing the Sea Pines Heritage Classic at Hilton Head Island and looked at the scoreboard, which indicated that a player had scored 86. 'No self-respecting pro should ever hit 86,' he sneered dismissively. The next day, a nervous and embarrassed Jones found himself with an eight-foot putt on the 18th to avoid an 86. He got away with an 85. The God of golf was feeling lenient.

In a similar manner, 17-year-old Seve Ballesteros opined to fellow pros the night before the 1974 Spanish Open that it is 'impossible for a pro golfer to shoot double figures on a single hole'. The next day, on the par-five ninth, Seve hit his first two shots out of bounds, his sixth into a lake, his next into a bunker and then two-putted. He scored 11.

— RIVER DEEP, MOUNTAIN HIGH —

The highest golf club in the world used to be the Tuctu Golf Club in Peru, where you could risk nausea, nosebleeds, headaches and worse as you teed off at the dizzying height of 14,335ft. That course is now abandoned, but here's a list of the current ten highest courses in the world.

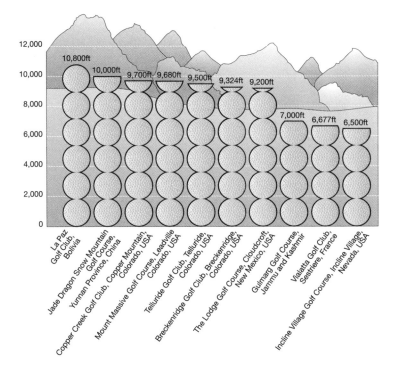

— EUROPEAN TOUR? —

The biggest and most important tour in the world after the USPGA Tour, the European Tour broke away from the PGA in 1971 to form a separate organisation. John Jacobs led the Tour until 1975, when he was succeeded by Ken Schofield, who, as executive director, has ran the Tour until his retirement at the beginning of the 2005 season.

Schofield was to a degree fortunate in the timing of his tenure, as players of the marketability and charisma of Seve Ballesteros, Bernhard Langer, Nick Faldo, Ian Woosnam and Sandy Lyle coincided with the early years of the Tour. Such players brought in their wake the sponsorship and popular support that the Tour required to increase its profile, along with the amount of prize money on offer and the number of tournaments staged. It all came together in 1985, when Europe dominated world golf. In that year, Langer won the Masters, with Seve tied in second place; Lyle won the British Open; and, most importantly for the Continent's standing in golf, Europe won the Ryder Cup at the Belfry, their first win on home soil for 28 years. Interest in golf soared and was given further impetus by the European Ryder Cup win at Muirfield Village two years later.

Since then the fortunes of the Tour have fluctuated, but the operation has generally flourished. Perhaps the most noticeable development over the years has been the geographical shift away from Europe. Of the 47 events staged in 2005, 18 (38 per cent) of the tournaments are actually not in Europe at all. In fact, the first 11 events are held in China, Hong Kong, South Africa, Singapore, Australia, New Zealand, Malaysia, USA and the Far East. The Tour then nips back to Europe for the Madeira Island Open in March, after which it heads halfway back across the world for the Indonesia Open.

The reasons for all this globe-hopping are partly climatic, of course, similar to the way in which the USPGA Tour has its West Coast Swing beginning in Hawaii and then following the sunshine through Florida, the Midwest and along the East Coast, respectively, as the summer creeps in.

The following list contains some of the venues for the 2005 European Tour, which in truth is more of a tour of the world:

> **25–8 November 2004** ....Chinese Open
>
> **2–5 December 2004** ....Hong Kong Open
>
> **20–3 January 2005** ....South African Open

27–30 January 2005 ....Singapore Caltex Masters

3–6 February 2005 ....Heineken Classic (Australia)

10–13 February 2005............Holden Open (New Zealand)

23–7 February 2005.....WGC–Accenture Matchplay (USA)

3–6 March 2005 ....Dubai Desert Classic

7–10 April 2005 ....Masters Tournament (USA)

12–15 May 2005 ....British Masters

23–6 June 2005 ....Open de France

21–4 July 2005 ....Players' Championship of Europe
(Germany)

11–14 August 2005 ....Russian Open

8–11 September 2005 ....German Masters

27–30 October 2005 ....Spanish Volvo Masters (Spain)

17–20 November 2005 ....WGC–Algarve World Cup
(Portugal)

— ALLISS' HALL OF FAME: PETER THOMSON —

A young Australian industrial chemist who turned pro at the age of 20, Peter Thomson had to leave his country in order to face top-class golfing competition. When he did so, he became the first man since Harry Vardon to win the British Open five times.

Thomson's game was perfectly suited to links golf. Although he wasn't a long hitter, he was deadly accurate and a player of subtle finesse shots who could read the undulating fairway of links courses with a sharp eye. He won his first British Open in 1954 at Royal Birkdale and won again in the following two years at St Andrews and Hoylake, respectively. He came second in 1957 at St Andrews to Bobby Locke, his great rival throughout the 1950s, but he made it four wins the next year after a playoff victory over DC Thomas at Royal Lytham.

From 1953 to 1958 Thomson played on the US Tour but managed only one win, the Texas Open, partly because he

— ALLISS' HALL OF FAME: PETER THOMSON (CONT'D) —

wasn't at ease with the length and differing requirements of US courses. The British Open, meanwhile, had been reinvigorated by the arrival of American players led by Arnold Palmer and Thomson's fifth victory in the competition came at Royal Birkdale in 1965, when he won against a field comprising the likes of Palmer, Nicklaus and Player.

Thomson also won on numerous occasions in Australia and New Zealand and can be seen as one of the first truly international golfing professionals, paving the way for the emergence of talented Australian players such as David Graham and Greg Norman. After his retirement, he turned to broadcasting and writing on golf (he is co-author of the much-respected *World Atlas Of Golf*) and to golf-related architecture.

— GOING GLOBAL —

In 1994, Greg Norman suggested the idea of a World Golf Tour with 10–12 tournaments per annum held around the world and paying huge prize money, competed for by the world's top 40 players. The concept was backed by Rupert Murdoch and supported by several top players, including Nick Price and Seve Ballesteros. Others, however, rejected the notion, 1995 US Ryder Cup captain Lanny Wadkins commenting, 'I think the public has seen enough greed from athletes.' The idea horrified the organisers of the US and European Tours, who believed with some justification that this proposal would devalue their own Tours and turn their tournaments into second-class events. It would also, they claimed, confuse the selection criteria for Ryder Cup teams, as it would be unclear how points would be allocated between the World Tour and other tournaments. When Norman's supporters realised the potential damage this could inflict on their livelihoods, many of them withdrew from the scheme and Norman, too, distanced himself from the idea.

However, Norman had started a ball rolling. In 1996, golf's five main professional Tours – the European Tour, the Japanese Golf Tour, the USPGA Tour, the PGA Tour of Australasia and the Southern African Tour – agreed to create new international events, beginning in 1999, to counter the threat of a World Tour. These events were to be jointly sanctioned under a new International Federation, with the Asian PGA Tour joining in 1999, and a worldwide ranking system was to be developed as a standard for entry.

The first three jointly sanctioned championships – the Accenture Match Play Championship, the NEC Invitational and the American Express Championship – were launched in 1999, with Jeff Maggert defeating Andrew Magee in a playoff in the Accenture tournament and Tiger Woods winning the other two. The World Cup began in December 2000 in Buenos Aires, Argentina, and was won by the US team of Woods and David Duval.

The World Golf Championship events feature players from around the world competing against one another in varied formats (matchplay, strokeplay and team) and offer some of the largest purses in professional golf, the winner in each event receiving in excess of $1 million. The Championships have been played on five different continents.

ACCENTURE MATCH PLAY CHAMPIONSHIP (JANUARY/FEBRUARY)
Format: Matchplay
Field: Top 64 available players, based on the Official World Golf Ranking

YEAR	LOCATION	CONTENDERS	WINNING MARGIN
1999	La Costa Resort and Spa, Carlsbad, California	Jeff Maggert def. Andrew Magee	38 holes
2000	La Costa Resort and Spa, Carlsbad, California	Darren Clarke def. Tiger Woods	4&3
2001	Metropolitan Golf Club, Victoria, Australia	Steve Stricker def. Pierre Fulke	2&1
2002	La Costa Resort and Spa, Carlsbad, California	Kevin Sutherland def. Scott McCarron	1 up
2003	La Costa Resort and Spa, Carlsbad, California	Tiger Woods def. David Toms	2&1
2004	La Costa Resort and Spa, Carlsbad, California	Tiger Woods def. Davis Love III	3&2

NEC INVITATIONAL (AUGUST)
Format: 72 holes, strokeplay, no cut.
Field: Playing members of the last-named United States and International Presidents Cup teams and the last-named United States and European Ryder Cup teams, if not otherwise eligible. Players ranked among the top 50 and ties on the Official World Golf Rankings as of Monday of tournament week, if not otherwise eligible.

— GOING GLOBAL (CONT'D) —

Tournament winners of worldwide events since the prior year's NEC Invitational with an Official World Golf Ranking strength of field rating of 100 points or more and, if not otherwise eligible, the winner of one selected tournament from each of the following Tours: Australasian Tour, Southern Africa Tour, Asian PGA and Japan Golf Tour.

Year	Location	Winner	Winning Score
1999	Firestone Country Club, Akron, Ohio	Tiger Woods	270
2000	Firestone Country Club, Akron, Ohio	Tiger Woods	259
2001	Firestone Country Club, Akron, Ohio	Tiger Woods	269
2002	Sahalee Country Club, Sammamish, Washington, DC	Craig Parry	268
2003	Firestone Country Club, Akron, Ohio	Darren Clarke	268
2004	Firestone Country Club, Akron, Ohio	Stewart Cink	269

AMERICAN EXPRESS CHAMPIONSHIP (SEPTEMBER/OCTOBER)
Format: 72 holes, strokeplay, no cut.
Field: 65–70 players, including the 44 of the top 50 from the Official World Ranking and leaders of the six Tours' Official Money Lists/Orders of Merit.

Year	Location	Winner	Winning Score
1999	Valderrama Golf Club, Valderrama, Spain	Tiger Woods	278
2000	Valderrama Golf Club, Valderrama, Spain	Mike Weir	277
2001	Bellerive Country Club, St Louis, Missouri (cancelled)		
2002	Mount Juliet Conrad Estate, Thomastown, Co Kilkenny, Ireland	Tiger Woods	263
2003	Capital City Club, Crabapple Course, Atlanta, Georgia	Tiger Woods	274
2004	Mount Juliet Conrad Estate, Thomastown, Co Kilkenny, Ireland	Ernie Els	270

WORLD CUP (NOVEMBER/DECEMBER)
Format: 72-hole team competition consisting of two rounds of fourball strokeplay and two rounds of foursome strokeplay, no cut.
Field: 24 two-man teams representing 24 countries.

YEAR	LOCATION	WINNING TEAM
2000	Buenos Aires Golf Club, Buenos Aires, Argentina	USA (Tiger Woods/David Duval)
2001	The Taiheiyo Club, Shizouka, Japan	South Africa (Ernie Els/Retief Goosen)
2002	Vista Vallarta, Puerto Vallarta, Mexico	Japan (Shigeki Maruyama/Toshi Izawa)
2003	The Ocean Course, Kiawah Island Resorts, South Carolina, USA	South Africa (Rory Sabbatini/Trevor Immelman)
2004	Real Club de Golf de Seville, Seville, Spain	England (Paul Casey/Luke Donald)

— ALLISS' HALL OF FAME: SAM SNEAD —

A poor farmer's son from the Virginia Hills, Samuel Jackson Snead won more tournaments on the US Tour than any other golfer. He was born in 1912, the same year as Byron Nelson and Ben Hogan, though his career long outlasted these other two greats. Known as 'Slammin' Sam' for the distance he could hit the ball, his smooth, effortless swing brought him 81 Tour victories in a career that lasted over four decades on the circuit.

A natural athlete as a youth, Snead chose golf over basketball and football and, after a spell of caddying at a local resort hotel in Virginia, he started his professional career in 1936. At his first tournament, the Hershey Open, he twice drove his opening tee shot out of bounds, his third attempt landing on the green, 350 yards away. In 1937 he won five times on Tour, including his first win at the Oakland Open. When he was shown a photo of himself in a New York newspaper, he commented, 'How in the world did they ever get that? I've never been to New York in my life.'

This tall figure, easily identified by his straw hat, his dry humour and his cocky grin, curiously never won the US Open

— ALLISS' HALL OF FAME: SAM SNEAD (CONT'D) —

(although he was runner-up on four occasions), but he won his first Major – the USPGA – in 1942, and again in 1952 and 1954. The Masters was his natural home (he won at Augusta in 1949, 1952 and 1954), and right up until his death in 2002 Snead would hit one of the opening ceremonial shots at the tournament. He also won the British Open at St Andrews in 1946, although he upset some locals when he first saw the Old Course and described it as 'an old abandoned golf course'.

Snead's healthy lifestyle (he was a non-smoker and modest drinker who kept physically fit) prolonged his career beyond that of most professionals. While he lost confidence in his putting later in his career, he still became the oldest player to win on Tour when, at the age of 52, he lifted the Greater Greensboro Open title for the eighth time – a record for a single tournament. In 1979 he set another record as the first player on Tour to shoot below his age when, at 67 years old, he shot a 66 at the Quad Cities Open. He was also instrumental in setting up the US Senior Tour.

— SIX TOP WOMEN GOLFERS (BESIDES ANNIKA) —

JOYCE WETHERED (1901–97)

Wethered was the woman of whom Bobby Jones said, 'I have never played with anyone…who made me feel so outclassed.' Gene Sarazen concurred, in 1997 describing her as 'the greatest woman golfer who ever lived'. Winner of five consecutive English Ladies' Amateur Championships between 1920 and 1924 and four British Ladies' Amateur Championships in the 1920s, Wethered could – as Jones discovered – hold her own with the men as well as the women. Indeed, at the peak of her career, her statistics could have earned her a place in the men's Walker Cup team. Her timing and concentration were faultless and, although she had a short backswing, she could hit the ball an astonishing distance. She retired after winning her third British Amateur title in 1925, but – now Lady Heathcote Amory – was lured back to the tournament in 1929 by the fact that it was played at St Andrews. In an epic match at that year's tournament, she won again, beating the legendary US Amateur champion Glenna Collett Vare on the 35th hole of the 36-hole championship, and retired for good thereafter. She was named head of the English Ladies' Golf Union in 1954 and died in Devon in 1997.

MICKEY WRIGHT (1935–)

With her technically perfect and rhythmic swing, Mickey Wright's length off the tee, coupled with her accurate shotmaking, enabled her to accumulate 82 titles on the US Ladies' Tour. In 1958 she won five tournaments, including the British Open and the LPGA, and by 1964 she had won 63 times on Tour, including four British Opens and four LPGAs. Her prowess on the golf course in the early 1960s was perhaps overshadowed by the intense competition between Jack Nicklaus and Arnold Palmer, who garnered most of the TV coverage, but she was fast becoming a legend in ladies' golf. Her immaculate ironplay and her ability to rescue herself from difficult situations on the course led to her becoming the most admired woman in the game. She stopped playing regularly in 1969 but came back from injury in 1973 to win the prestigious Dinah Shore event, and she played her last tournament in 1980. In 1999, Associated Press named her Female Golfer of the Century.

LAURA DAVIES (1963–)

An easygoing, powerfully built woman, with a passion for soccer and fast cars, Laura Davies is the finest woman golfer Britain has produced. A prodigious hitter of the ball, with a crisp and accurate short game, her first big international success came when she won the US Women's Open in 1987, although she wasn't a member of the USPGA Tour of that year, being granted full Tour status without the need to qualify.

By 1994, Davies was unquestionably the world's top female golfer, winning on an unprecedented five different Tours – three events in the US, two in Europe and one each in Thailand, Japan and Australia. Between 1994 and 1996, she won 23 events across the world, and in 1997 she became the first woman to win a LPGA event – the Standard Register Ping – four years in succession. In 2003 she picked up her 45th international win, claiming the ANZ Ladies' Masters on the Evian Tour.

Davies is the only player to have competed in all eight Solheim Cups and shares the all-time points record with Annika Sorenstam. She is particularly remembered in the tournament for her stirring captaincy in 1982, when she won all three of her games at Dalmahoy and inspired Europe to defeat the USA.

NANCY LOPEZ (1957–)

Nancy Lopez set the world of US women's golf alight in 1978, when, in her rookie year on Tour, she won no fewer than nine events – five of them back to back – and was voted both Rookie of the Year and Player of the Year. A dashing figure with a seemingly permanent smile, she quickly became a favourite on Tour, her uninhibited strokeplay and her dark good looks

— SIX TOP WOMEN GOLFERS (BESIDES ANNIKA) —
(CONT'D)

bringing in the crowds in much the same way as Arnold Palmer had done for the men's game.

In 1979, a further eight victories saw Lopez once again claim the title of Player of the Year, and by 1983 her unorthodox but highly effective swing helped her amass over $1 million in career earnings. Her fourth Player of the Year award came in 1988, and she has won the LPGA Championship three times, although, curiously, never the US Open. She has been runner-up four times in the British Open, most recently in 1997, when she shot four rounds in the 60s but still finished one stroke behind winner Alison Nicholas. That year she also won her 48th and last title on Tour – the Chick-fil-A Charity – and passed the $5 million mark in her career earnings.

KATHY WHITWORTH (1939–)

During the mid-1960s, Whitworth was undisputedly the leading female golfer in the world, winning on the US LPGA Tour eight times in 1965, nine times in 1966, eight times in 1967 and ten times in 1968. She joined the Tour in 1958 and won her first title, the Kelly's Girls' Open, in 1962. By the time she'd left the Tour, in the late 1980s, she had accumulated 88 wins – more than any other golfer, male or female, in history. Her 40-foot winning putt on the 72nd hole of the Women's Kemper Open in 1983 tied her with Sam Snead's total of 84, and she overtook Snead's record at the next year's Rochester International.

Whitworth's ungainly but hugely effective and consistent swing earned her the leading money spot eight times and she was named Golfer of the Decade by *Golf Magazine* for the period 1968–77. She won the LPGA Championship but never managed to claim the British Open title, although her third place in 1981 saw her become the first woman to earn more than $1 million in career earnings. She captained the US Solheim Cup team in 1990 and 1992 and now competes on the Women's Senior Tour.

PATTY BERG (1918–)

An all-round athlete who took up golf at the age of 13, Patty Berg had an outstanding career as an amateur, winning 28 championships, including the US Women's Open. Sponsored by Wilson's Sporting Goods company (with whom she still maintains a relationship), Berg turned professional in 1940, compensating for the relative lack of tournaments in that year by giving exhibitions and clinics. In 1941, she suffered a broken knee in a car crash and was out of the game for eighteen months, but she returned in 1943, winning two tournaments before joining the Marines as a lieutenant. In 1946 she won the British Open, and by the time she won her last tournament, in 1962, she had collected 57 victories, 15 of them Majors.

Berg became first president of the US LPGA in 1950 and was leading money-winner on Tour in 1954, 1955 and 1957. She has received numerous awards and citations, including being named as one the 50 best golfers of all time by *Golf Magazine* in 2000. The Tour established the Patty Berg Award in 1978 for 'outstanding contribution to women's golf'.

— THE GREAT BATTLES OF GOLF HISTORY 4 —

SEVE BALLESTEROS V NICK PRICE, BRITISH OPEN, LYTHAM, 1988
Before this contest, the erratic but supremely gifted Ballesteros had already achieved legendary status with his two Masters and two Open titles, as well as his numerous other victories throughout the world. His craft and flamboyance, however, were to be tested at Lytham by South Africa's Nick Price, a level-headed, popular and worthy opponent.

Heavy rain on the Lancashire coast had led to the postponement of the last day's play until the Monday, with a relatively modest crowd in attendance. At tee-off on the final round, Price led Ballesteros and Nick Faldo by two strokes, though Faldo's challenge faded at the long seventh hole, where he parred but where his two companions both claimed eagles. Ballesteros then dramatically birdied the next six holes, and by the turn the Spaniard was two ahead of Price. By the 16th tee they were level again, but Ballesteros, after a splendidly executed nine-iron pitch, sneaked ahead, and although Price recovered brilliantly from the rough at the 17th, he remained one stroke behind.

On the final hole, Ballesteros left Price with a putt to level, but the South African overhit, leaving the Spanish genius to claim another Major. His final-round 65 – 'the best of my life' – set a record for the British Open, while with his final 69 Price became the only man ever in the tournament to have broken par on every round. Ballesteros remarked of Price's performance, 'It's a pity that there is only one champion.'

— LIGHTNING STRIKE —

One of the most uncomfortable moments on a golf course is when the unmistakeable sound of thunder is heard, heralding the imminent threat of lightning. There are few places to shelter on the average course, and perhaps the best tip is to take off one's shoes, make sure the clubs are a good distance away, sit in a bunker and hope – or to make one's way with all possible speed back to the clubhouse. The Tottenham Hotspur and Scotland international footballer John White was struck and killed by lightning at Crews Hill GC, north London, in 1964 as he sheltered under a tree. More recently, at the 1975 Western Open near Chicago, Lee Trevino, Bobby Nichols and Jerry Heard were on the 13th hole when lightning struck nearby. Trevino, leaning against his golf bag, was thrown into the air and his back was burned. Heard, also thrown into the air, suffered a burnt groin. Nichols, holding an eight-iron and with a steel plate in his head, was knocked backwards. All three golfers were hospitalised and Trevino and Nichols withdrew from the tournament. Heard completed the tournament and finished in third place. It took all three golfers months to regain their form.

— DOUBLE HIT —

At the 1985 US Open at Oakland Hills, Michigan, TC Chen was four strokes ahead at the fifth hole on the final round. He chipped onto the green but hit the ball twice, first on impact and then on follow-through, incurring a two-stroke penalty. He ended up with a quadruple-bogey eight on the hole and finished up in second place to Andy North. Thereafter, he was known as 'Two Chip' Chen.

— ANIMAL INTRUSIONS —

Birdies and eagles are a staple part of golf, but other birds and animals have been associated with the game. Here are just a few examples.

- Eleven-year-old Willie Fraser from Kingussie GC in the Highlands of Scotland, playing on 12 August ('The Glorious Twelfth') killed a grouse with his tee shot. The hapless bird had probably been relieved to have just escaped from the adjacent field's shotguns.

- In 1934, at St Margaret's-on-Cliffe, Kent, club pro WJ Robinson hit a cow on the head with his tee shot at the 18th. The animal staggered on for 50 yards or so and then dropped dead.

- At the 1972 Singapore Open, Jimmy Stewart approached his ball only to find it guarded by a cobra. He killed the cobra with his club, killed its mate who had crawled out to find the source of the commotion, and then continued with his round.

- At the 1968 British Open at Carnoustie, John Morgan was bitten by a rat while searching for his ball in the rough. Shaken by the incident, he carded a 92.

- The Talamore Golf Course in Pinehurst, North Carolina, opened in 1991. Instead of a normal caddie, the club offered the services of llamas, which could each carry two golf bags.

- While playing St Andrews in May 1934, the future 1940 US Open champion Lawson Little hit the green at the infamous 17th hole, but then a Persian cat ran on, picked up the ball and ran away with it. Little was awarded a free drop.

— USPGA TOUR HOBBY OF THE YEAR —

Asking people how they spend their leisure time is always difficult, particularly if the information is intended for publication. Even if we felt the urge, few of us would admit that we enjoy ripping off spiders' legs or punching holes in car tyres. Blandness is important in order to camouflage hidden desires, so the following information is to be treated with some scepticism.

There are those who claim that the USPGA Tour is made up of golfers who are conservative, Republican-voting, family-loving Christians imbued with the good old values of the USA – which, of course, includes killing animals for sport. Well, there is some truth in this assertion, if one looks at the 'Personal Interests' section of the 2004 *Tour Handbook*, where a staggering number of these people list 'hunting and fishing' as their major off-course pre-occupations, beginning (alphabetically) with Fulton Allem and ending with Tiger Woods. The list ends with Richard Zukol's main interest, 'studying the human mind', so perhaps all is not lost.

The usual wealthy US sportsman's hobbies – racing cars, flying, fast boats, skiing and so on – are also evident, with several golfers going to extreme lengths to forget the pressures of the testing putt; Jay Don Blake and Kenny Perry, for instance, are fans of drag racing, while Scott Gump favours white-water rafting, DJ Brigman is an aficionado of sky diving and Cliff Kresge spends his leisure time 'wind-tunnel flying', whatever that is, although it sounds terrifying and makes David Edwards' passion for radio-controlled miniature cars appear positively wimpish. Jonathan Kaye also bucks the macho trend by describing himself as an 'avid indoorsman', which makes you want to shake his hand in relief after the constant litany of 'hunting, fishing, cars', etc.

Elsewhere on the list, players opt for the traditional means of passing time, with music (usually unspecified, although 'Christian music' in the case of Lee Janzen), reading (comics? John Grisham? Stock Exchange reports?), the family ('being a great dad', asserts Dennis Paulson proudly) and Christianity. Indeed, Bible study and 'church activities' are the spiritual refuge of some of these millionaires, including Scott Simpson, Spike McRoy, Pat Bates and David Ogrin. Others prefer the less spiritual pursuits of the gourmet life, and these include Michael Allan (something of an intellectual polymath with interests in wine, reading, politics and – of course – motorcycles), Kelly Gibson

('Cajun food'), Tag Ridings ('down-home cooking'), Duffy Waldorf ('wine collecting'), Bob Burns ('beer brewing') and Tripp Isenhour ('gourmet cooking'). They are all trumped, however, by David Frost, whose finest pleasure is obtained from 'good food and wine from his own vineyard'. Beat that.

There are also some rather other odd pastimes indulged in by these sporting gods, and it comes as no surprise to discover that Jesper Parnevik heads this particular list with an entry that begins, 'Magic, vitamins, bridge...' Donnie Hammond, meanwhile, favours 'astronomy', Todd Hamilton 'crossword puzzles', Steve Elkington 'caricature drawing' and Andrew Magee 'whistling'. Chris Smith goes one stage further than Magee, his entry reading 'rodeo, whistling show tunes', but presumably not at the same time. A few Tour members even spend their leisure hours in socially beneficial activities; Brad Faxon and Billy Andrade, for instance, run a children's charity that has so far raised over $4 million, while Kirk Triplett busies himself with children's adoption matters.

The time has come, however, to award the prize for Hobby of the Year. In third place is Rich Barcelo, whose hobby of 'playing with his dogs', unless it's a euphemism for something more sinister, is just too sad to keep him out of the winning circle. Runner-up is Brian Bateman, who, instead of blasting deer to pieces, prefers the rather more sedate pastime of 'watching the Three Stooges'. And the winner, ladies and gentlemen, is Robert Gamez, whose unique and touching diversion from the three-iron is 'going to Disney theme parks'. Your Mickey Mouse golf visor is on its way, Bob.

— FORGETFULNESS —

Three-time British Open winner and South African master putter Bobby Locke was 3ft from the pin on the 72nd hole at the 1957 British Open with a three-stroke lead over Peter Thomson in second place. He had to mark his ball to allow his playing companion to putt. Locke measured off one putter's length, his head cocked to the side, then removed his ball and marked it. When it was his turn to putt, he forgot he had moved the ball and played from the marked position, sinking his putt and winning his fourth British Open title. The Champions Committee pointed out his breach of the rules but decided that he had gained no advantage and the winning score stood, an unusual but welcome example of lenience from officialdom.

— ALLISS' HALL OF FAME: SEVE BALLESTEROS —

When a smiling, 19-year-old Spaniard teed off at the 1976 British Open at Royal Birkdale, no one in the crowd knew that they were watching the man who was to become the dominant force in European golf for the next 15 years. His elegant swing and rhythmic follow-through marked him out as a special golfer, and although he was often wild off the tee, his ability to play brilliant recovery shots, his sublime short game and his decisive putting propelled him to greatness.

Seve Ballesteros grew up in a small village in Spain and practised his game by hitting stones with a makeshift three-iron on the beach. He then became a caddie and was playing off scratch by the age of 13 before turning pro in 1974 and playing on the 1975 European Tour.

In the 1976 British Open, Ballesteros came second to Johnny Miller after holding the lead for two rounds, and in the following two years he won the European Order of Merit. Three years later he claimed his first Major at Royal Lytham, where he finished three shots ahead of Ben Crenshaw and Jack Nicklaus, while in 1980 he conquered America, becoming the first European and youngest player to win the Masters. In 1983 he won the Masters again, four shots ahead of Ben Crenshaw and Tom Kite, and in the following year he won the British Open for a second time, beating Tom Watson at St Andrews with a birdie on the final hole. He secured his third British Open title in 1988, scoring a blistering final-round 65 to see off the challenge of Nick Price at Royal Lytham.

Ballesteros's flair, flamboyance and breathtaking shot-making were allied to a steeliness of will and unflinching determination to prove himself the best. His successes in America, combined with his heroic performances in the Ryder Cup alongside compatriot José Maria Olazábal, proved to European golf that the Americans were not impregnable. The likes of Faldo, Langer, Woosnam and Olazábal followed the trail Ballesteros blazed by also winning Masters championships.

Ballesteros continued to play in the Ryder Cup until 1995 and was appointed non-playing captain in 1997 at Valderrama, where his eccentric and enthusiastic leadership helped to motivate Europe to a 14.5–13.5 win over the USA, and in 2000 he introduced the Seve Trophy to the European Tour schedule. While his form has slumped dramatically in recent years, he remains an iconic figure in the world of international golf, having won 72 tournaments worldwide in his stellar career.

— GOLF ON THE MOON —

In May 1961 Alan Shepard Jr became the first American in space. He set another record ten years later when he commanded Apollo 14 on the first Moon landing. Having spent a day and a half on the Moon's surface collecting rocks and carrying out scientific experiments, Shepard took out a collapsible, makeshift six-iron and hit two golf balls. Encumbered by a space suit and thick gloves, but aided by the moon's gravity being one-sixth that of the Earth, he hit the second ball for what he described as 'miles and miles and miles' (later downgraded to just over 200 yards). The R&A telegrammed him as follows: 'Warmest congratulations to you and your colleagues on your great achievement and safe return. Please refer to Rules of Golf section on etiquette, paragraph 6, quote, before leaving a bunker a player should carefully fill up and smooth over all holes and footprints made by him, unquote.'

— ANOTHER 'STUPID' —

Australian Kel Nagle, winner of the 1960 British
Open along with 27 other tournaments, opened the
Alcan Golfer of the Year event with a perfectly
respectable 70. His marker, however, inadvertently
marked the score for his first round – 35 – in the
space on Nagle's scorecard reserved for his score on
the ninth hole. Nagle signed his card without noticing
this and, given that a golfer is responsible for the
accuracy of his scorecard, his total score moved from
70 to 105. He finished last in the tournament.

— MEMBERS ONLY —

Discrimination has been an unfortunate aspect of golf since the emergence of
private clubs. The position of black golfers has been particularly controversial,
especially in the USA. As long ago as the second US Open, held at Shinnecock
Hills in 1896, the issue of racism was highlighted when a black golfer and
caddie at the club, John Shippen, entered the competition and the remainder
of the field – all white British immigrants – threatened to withdraw rather than
play with a black man. Theodore Havemeyer, owner of the American Sugar
Company and the major financier of the British Open, replied that they could
do what they wanted, but the competition would go ahead with Shippen in
the field. The players relented and Shippen played. Tied for the lead after the
first round in the 36-hole, one-day tournament, he took an 11 at a par four
in the second round and ended in fifth place.

In the early years of the 20th century, it was difficult for black players to
compete, partly for economic reasons. In 1925, the US Colored Golfers'
Association was formed (later changing their name to the United Golfers'
Association in 1929) and funded intermittent tournaments, usually for much
less lucrative prize funds than the white-dominated Tour. The situation was
compounded by the clause inserted in 1916 in the USPGA Constitution that
quite explicitly stated that non-Caucasians could not be members of the Tour.
The clause was revoked in 1961, when California made it illegal to stage PGA
tournaments on courses where blacks were excluded.

The first black person to play on Tour after this ruling was Charlie Sifford,
whose ball was repeatedly kicked into the rough by fans while he received
threatening calls and death threats and had to pull out of the Greensboro
Open because of racist heckling, although he did go on to win the Hartford

Open in 1967 and the Los Angeles Open in 1969. The greatest player of modern times, Tiger Woods, has said, 'The pain, suffering and sacrifice experienced by Mr Sifford in being a lonely pioneer for black golfers on the PGA Tour will never be forgotten by me.' Sifford was joined on Tour in 1967 by Lee Elder, whose win at the 1974 Monsanto Open made him eligible for the 1975 Masters, where he became the first African-American to compete in the tournament. He was also the first black player to participate in the Ryder Cup, in 1979.

Shoal Creek in Birmingham, Alabama, was selected as the venue for the USPGA Championship in 1990, and when asked about discrimination at the club, a representative of Shoal Creek, Hall Thompson, stated, 'We don't discriminate in every other area except the blacks,' revealing somewhat messily the club's policy of admitting only whites as members. A furore erupted over his remarks, with Civil Rights groups protesting and sponsors withdrawing their advertising. Shortly before the tournament, the club admitted their first black member, Louis Willie, albeit on an honorary basis, and the competition went ahead. The USPGA stated that there would be no more tournaments held under their auspices at clubs that discriminated on the basis of race. Later that year, Augusta National also signed up their first black member.

Augusta was again in the news in 2003, this time over the issue of sexual discrimination. Augusta was an elite, 300-member club that, in its 69-year history, had never had a woman member. Indeed, there was no waiting list, as potential members could not apply; they had to be invited. Championed by *The New York Times*, which ran 102 stories featuring her in the run-up to the Masters, Martha Burk of the National Council of Women's Organisations launched a campaign accusing the club of 'gender apartheid' and saying that it, and its chairman William 'Hootie' Johnson had a 'moral obligation' to allow women members. Johnson replied by saying that, under the first Amendment to the US Constitution, Augusta, as a private club, had a legal right to associate freely with whoever it wished. Burk's attempt to stage a demonstration outside the Masters fizzled out, with only 40 demonstrators turning up, but the issue led to a huge story nationally in the weeks running up to the tournament and Burk did women's golf a favour by highlighting it.

There are still many clubs in the USA and Britain where women are not full members, cannot vote at AGMs, have restricted tee times and are banned from certain parts of the clubhouse, although Tiger Woods' arrival has greatly helped the cause of non-discrimination by race. It would be nice to think that this other reactionary and just as discriminatory side of golf will soon be a distant and distasteful memory.

— PLAYING THE BRITISH OPEN COURSES —

ST ANDREWS OLD COURSE

Par 72 (6,609 yards)
Shortest hole: eighth, 'Short' (166 yards)
Longest hole: 14th, 'Long' (523 yards)
Course record: 62 (Curtis Strange, Dunhill Cup, 1987)

Renowned throughout the world as the home of golf, the Old Course at St Andrews has hosted the British Open no fewer than 26 times, including the 2005 event. Nestling in the northeast corner of Fife, between the old, historic buildings of the town of St Andrews and the Tay estuary, the Old Course has hosted golf since 1400. By 1764 the course contained 22 holes – 11 out and 11 back – and this was later shortened to 18, setting the standard for the game. The Society of St Andrews' Golfers was formed in 1754 and was changed to the Royal and Ancient Golf Club in 1834, under the patronage of King William IV.

The Old Course is a public links run since 1974 by the St Andrews Links Trust, which also oversees its five neighbouring courses. It's a course that has evolved naturally, featuring seven enormous double greens and a huge number of bunkers designed to trap the unwary.

MEMORABLE MOMENT
Doug Sanders missing a 30in putt for victory at the 72nd hole in the 1970 British Open and being forced to a playoff with Jack Nicklaus that Nicklaus won.

MUIRFIELD

Par 71 (6,963 yards)
Shortest hole: 13th (159 yards)
Longest hole: fifth (559 yards)
Course record: 64 (Rodger David, British Open, 1987)

Under the ownership of the Honourable Company of Edinburgh Golfers, Muirfield, in east Lothian, first played host to the British Open in 1892, the first year the tournament was held over 72 holes. Laid out in two compact loops, with the anti-clockwise back nine within the clockwise outer nine, the course is a supreme test of driving skill and shotmaking. Anything wayward will be punished, either by the clinging rough or the bunkers, which are designed to ensnare all wayward shots. Jack Nicklaus, who won the Open here in 1966, was so impressed with the course that he named his own course in Dublin, Ohio, Muirfield Village.

MEMORABLE MOMENT

Nick Faldo's second shot with a five-iron to the heart of the green at the 72nd hole in the 1987 British Open to defeat Paul Azinger.

ROYAL TROON

Par 74 (7,265 yards)
Shortest hole: eighth (126 yards)
Longest hole: sixth (599 yards)
Course record: 64 (Greg Norman, British Open, 1989)

Owing its formation in 1878 to the development of the national network of railways in the 19th century, Troon nestles between the main Glasgow-to-Ayr line and the Firth of Clyde. The course contains both the longest and shortest holes in the British Open championship. The opening six holes are away from the clubhouse, following the shoreline, while the next six loop around at the far end of the course and the finishing six return towards the clubhouse, normally into a stiff wind. It is these final six holes where reputations normally suffer.

MEMORABLE MOMENT

Greg Norman's drive at the 18th into a fairway bunker in a four-hole playoff against Mark Calcavecchia in the 1989 British Open. This miscalculation, and his subsequent shot against the face of the bunker, cost him the title. Earlier in the day Norman had shot the course record of 64.

TURNBERRY

Par 70 (6,976 yards)
Shortest hole: 11th, 'Maidens' (174 yards)
Longest hole: 17th, 'Lang Whang' (597 yards)
Course record: 63 (Greg Norman, British Open, 1986)

Set against the spectacularly beautiful background of the Firth of Clyde, the Isle of Arran and Ailsa Crag, the Ailsa Course at Turnberry staged its first British Open in 1977. It was first opened in 1909 and, after two stints as an aerodrome, was redesigned by MacKenzie Ross and reopened in 1951. The first eight holes are played alongside the edge of the ocean, while the back nine are more inland and generally into the wind. The clubhouse was completely refurbished in recent years and is now one of the most striking in Britain. Colin Montgomerie's Links Golf Academy is a feature of Turnberry.

MEMORABLE MOMENT

The unforgettable 'Duel in the Sun' at the 1977 British Open between Tom Watson and Jack Nicklaus that Watson won.

— PLAYING THE BRITISH OPEN COURSES (CONT'D) —

CARNOUSTIE

Par 70 (6,992 yards)
Shortest hole: 13th, 'Whins' (141 yards)
Longest hole: sixth, 'Long' (500 yards)
Course record: 65 (Jack Newton, British Open, 1975)

Situated on the northern shore of the Firth of Tay, Carnoustie Golf Club was formed in 1842, converted to 18 holes by Old Tom Morris in 1867 and revamped by James Braid in 1926. It has been home to some of the great British Opens, including Ben Hogan's win in 1953, Gary Player's victory in 1968 and Tom Watson's first Major in 1975. Thereafter the course fell into disrepair and neglect but was refurbished to host the British Open again in 1999. The course is renowned as being long and tough, although not particularly visually attractive, and possesses fearsome pot bunkers as well as two burns that criss-cross fairways and guard some of the greens. Carnoustie is a real test, particularly when the wind blows in from the estuary, which is most of the time.

MEMORABLE MOMENT
Jean Van de Velde taking his socks off and shooting a seven at the final hole of the 1999 British Open to throw away his lead and the title.

ROYAL LYTHAM AND ST ANNES

Par 71 (6,673 yards)
Shortest hole: ninth (144 yards)
Longest hole: seventh (544 yards)
Course record: 65 (Christy O'Connor, British Open 1969, subsequently matched by Brian Huggett, Bill Longmuir and Seve Ballesteros)

A somewhat physically unprepossessing golf course when compared to some of the great Scottish links, Lytham is ringed by, on one side, suburban Victorian housing and, on the other, the railway line. However, this Lancashire course has seen some of the great British Open championships, from Bobby Jones's first win in 1926 to Gary Player's triumph in 1974 and Seve Ballesteros's second victory at Lytham in 1988. Although softer in feel than, for instance, Carnoustie, it's certainly not as easy a course as it might initially appear, with the first four and the last five holes reckoned to be among the trickiest in English golf.

MEMORABLE MOMENT
Tony Jacklin sinking his final putt on the 18th to win the 1969 British Open, the first British victory in the tournament since Max Faulkner in 1951.

ROYAL BIRKDALE

Par 72 (6,690 yards)
Shortest hole: seventh (150 yards)
Longest hole: 15th (542 yards)
Club record: 64 (Mark O'Meara)

Eight times host of the British Open, Royal Birkdale on the Lancashire coast was created in 1889 and the existing links were developed in 1922. The club held its first British Open in 1954, with Peter Thomson the winner. Although its fairways are flat, without the undulations of typical links courses, and its greens clearly observable, the many fairway bunkers and the rough mean that accuracy is imperative. Arnold Palmer won his first Open title here in 1961, and other great winners have included Tom Watson and Lee Trevino.

MEMORABLE MOMENT
Lee Trevino recovering from his seven at the 71st to beat Lu Liang Huan by one shot on the 72nd for the British Open title.

ROYAL ST GEORGE'S

Par 70 (6,860 yards)
Shortest hole: sixth (155 yards)
Longest hole: seventh (530 yards)
Course record: 64 (Tony Jacklin, Dunlop Masters, 1967, subsequently matched by Christy O'Connor Jr and Greg Norman)

Nestling next to the quaint Kentish harbour town of Sandwich, Royal St George's is rich in golfing history. The club was formed in 1887 and the course was originally composed of tall sand dunes and blind carries, although this has now been modified. In 1934 Henry Cotton shot a 65 here on his way to winning the first British Open trophy to be lifted by an Englishman since 1923, and Sandy Lyle earned a similar victory in 1985, ending a 16-year hiatus for British golfers.

MEMORABLE MOMENT
Greg Norman equalling the course record of 64 on the final day of the 1993 British Open to win the tournament by two strokes over Nick Faldo. Bernhard Langer, playing with Norman, described it as the finest round he'd ever seen.

— ALLISS' HALL OF FAME: TIGER WOODS —

Named after his father's comrade in the Vietnam War, Eldrick 'Tiger' Woods was a child and youth prodigy, appearing with his putter on *The Bob Hope Show* at the age of three (at the same age, he broke 50 for nine holes), a club champion at eight, US Junior champion at 15, and US Amateur Champion an unprecedented three years running between 18 and 21.

The long-hitting, nerveless and deadly accurate Woods made his professional debut on the USPGA Tour in 1996 at the Milwaukee Open, where he smashed his opening tee shot over 330 yards. That year he entered eight Tour events and won two, while the following year he won another four, including the Masters, where he ended an incredible 12 strokes ahead of second-placed Tom Kite and became the youngest ever Masters winner, and his final score of 270 set a tournament scoring record. He won seven tournaments in 1998 and another eight in 1999, including the USPGA, and that year he set a record in official earnings (over $6.5 million) while leading the Tour in stroke average, total driving, greens in regulation, birdies and all-round ranking.

The 24-year-old phenom had a brilliant season in 2000, winning three of the four Majors along with the Canadian Open and four other USPGA Tour events to collect a total of over $9.5 million in Tour earnings. The following year, he won the Masters again (along with four Tour titles) to become the first player in history to hold all four Majors at the same time, and in 2002 he again won the Masters and US Open, adding for good measure the WGC–American Express Championship.

At the time of writing, however, Woods has gone ten Majors without a win, amid talk of a slump in form. Certainly, his accurate driving appears to have deserted him and his game is redeemed by the excellence of his putting and his short game generally. In autumn 2004 he was overtaken by Vijay Singh and Ernie Els in the World Rankings. Perhaps his enormous wealth from sponsorship is dulling his ambition, or maybe his body is succumbing to the demands placed on it by his massively powerful swing. Even so, only a very brave man would bet against Tiger soon re-assuming his position as the game's dominant force and possibly the greatest player of all time.

— WODEHOUSE ON GOLF —

PG Wodehouse (1881–1975) is, of course, best known for creating the hapless, feckless Bertie Wooster and his unflappable, manipulative manservant, Jeeves. Wodehouse was also, however, a prolific writer on golf, and his book *The Golf Omnibus*, first published in 1975, is still in print today. It's a collection of 31 short stories, set in the 1920s and 1930s, with titles such as 'The Heart Of A Goof', The Awakening Of Rollo Podmarsh', 'Those In Peril On The Tee' and 'The Salvation of George Mackintosh', all narrated by the Oldest Member, whose has a disconcerting habit of bearding young club members and offering sage advice through relevant reminiscences.

The Oldest Member is of the view that golf teaches humility, self-reliance, independence of mind and a deep humanitarian spirit, and he never tires of reminding his often reluctant listeners of this. The perfect antidote to youthful romantic entanglements and unrequited love (the theme underlying virtually all the stories), golf can soothe the savage breast and resolve even the most complex emotional difficulties and relationships. The stories in *The Golf Omnibus* are among the most inventive and funniest in the literature of golf, and Wodehouse's laconic asides and comments are gems of golfing wit. Here are a few choice selections from the book:

> 'I attribute the insane arrogance of the later Roman emperors almost entirely to the fact that, never having played golf, they never knew that chastening humility which is engendered by a topped chip-shot. If Cleopatra had been ousted in the first round of the Ladies' Singles, we would have heard a lot less of her proud imperiousness.'

> 'There were three things in the world that he held in the smallest esteem – slugs, poets and caddies with hiccups.'

> 'Golf is the Great Mystery. Like some capricious goddess, it bestows its favours with what would appear an almost fat-headed lack of method and discrimination. On every side we see two big-fisted he-men floundering around in three figures, stopping every few minutes to let through little shrimps with

— WODEHOUSE ON GOLF (CONT'D) —

knock-knees and hollow cheeks, who are tearing off snappy seventy-fours. Giants of finance have to accept a stroke from their junior clerks. Men capable of governing empires fail to control a small, white ball which presents no difficulties to others with one ounce more brain than a cuckoo-clock. Mysterious, but there it is.'

'It was a morning when all nature shouted, "Fore!" The breeze, as it blew gently up from the valley, seemed to bring a message of hope and cheer, whispering of chip-shots holed and brassies landing squarely on the meat. The fairway, as yet unscarred by the irons of a hundred dubs, smiled greenly up at the azure sky; and the sun, peeping above the trees, looked like a giant golf-ball perfectly lofted by the mashie of some unseen god and about to drop dead by the pin of the 18th. It was the day of the opening of the course after the long winter, and a crowd of considerable dimensions had collected at the first tee. Plus fours gleamed in the sunshine, and the air was charged with happy anticipation.'

In his introduction to the anthology, written when he was 92 years old, Wodehouse laments the commercialisation of modern golf compared with the game in old days, when 'to be a good golfer you had to be Scottish, preferably with a name like Sandy McHoots or Jock Auchtermuchty... Of such as these the bard has said, "Hech thrawfu' raltie rorkie, wi' thecht ta' croonie clapperhead and fash wi' unco' pawkie."' Although clearly a traditionalist, Wodehouse understood the enduring fascination of golf and, to his credit, its often pointless and hilarious absurdity. Although the oldest story, 'The Clicking Of Cuthbert', was written in 1916, *The Golf Omnibus* remains as fresh and sparkling today as the early-morning frost on the first tee.

— LONG SHORT HOLE —

The ninth hole at Portal Golf Club is only 125 yards long and yet can take at least 65 minutes to play. Why? Because the tee is in Saskatchewan, Canada, which doesn't observe daylight saving time, and the green is in the US state of North Dakota, which does. For six months of the year, the time difference between tee and hole is one hour.

— THE GREAT BATTLES OF GOLF HISTORY 5 —

NICK FALDO V GREG NORMAN, THE MASTERS, AUGUSTA, 1996

Perhaps the most public and excruciatingly protracted collapse in the history of top-level sport – never mind golf – was Greg Norman's demolition by a magnificently determined Nick Faldo in the final round at Augusta in 1996.

After being assured by a leading golf journalist, 'Even you can't fuck up now, Greg,' referring to his habit of snatching defeat from the jaws of victory, Norman strode onto the first tee with a six-stroke lead over Faldo. However, the press don't always get it right, and a shocked and largely silent crowd observed a steely Faldo, and a clearly increasingly flustered Norman, arrive at the 12th hole all square, with the White Shark having thrown away his apparently unassailable advantage.

Worse was to follow for Norman, and his game proceeded to fall apart. At the 12th, he hit his tee shot into the creek (two down), then found the water again at the 16th (four down). Meanwhile, Faldo was playing some superbly consistent golf and piling the mental pressure on the increasingly desperate Australian. TV viewers and the Augusta crowd watched with a mixture of sympathy and disbelief as Faldo birdied the 18th for a 67 and a five-shot victory over Norman, a swing of an amazing 11 strokes over the round.

Norman, an under-achiever despite his Majors and tournament wins across the world, was yet again found wanting when it mattered most, finishing with 78, his eighth second-place finish in a Major tournament. 'I don't know what to say,' said Faldo to Norman when the game ended; 'I just want to give you a hug.' Norman later explained, 'My swing had gone to a place I didn't know and I couldn't retrieve it.'

— CADDIE TALES —

Stories about caddies are legion. Many are apocryphal but none the less revealing for that. Here's a choice selection.

A group of wealthy Middle-Eastern gentlemen, dressed in Arab attire, play a round at St Andrews and, after holing at the 18th, one of them presents his caddie with a generous tip. 'Thank you very much, sir,' replies the caddie. 'I hope your head gets better soon.'

Still at St Andrews, a duffer from the USA hacks his way round the Old Course and, almost inevitably, ends up in the dreaded Road Hole bunker beside the 17th green. After several fruitless attempts to remove the ball, he despairingly turns to his caddie and says, 'What do I take from here?' The caddie replies, 'What about the 7:30 to Dundee?'

US pro Julius Boros, whose regular caddie failed to turn up, began a competition by picking out a young boy from the gallery to take over the role. After his second shot on the first hole, he said to the boy. 'Pick up the divot, kid.' As the round progressed, the young caddie was increasingly tailing back from Boros and seemed to be in difficulties. 'Are you OK, son?' asked Boros. 'Yes, sir, but what do you want me to do with these?' he said, emptying a pile of divots from Boros's golf bag.

An American golfer, visiting a Scottish golf links for the first time, was enthusing to his caddie about the beauty of the heather, gorse and scenery, the delights of the links game, and the charming people he had met on his trip. 'Above all,' he said, 'the game is so friendly,' to which the caddie responded, 'It wasn't supposed to be.'

During a particularly trying round that involved much criss-crossing of the fairways, visits to the whins and gorse and extended stays in bunkers, a golfer asked his caddie, 'Do you think I can get there with a five-iron?' The caddie replied, 'Eventually, sir.'

— ALLISS' HALL OF FAME: TOM WATSON —

A slightly built psychology graduate from Missouri, Tom Watson was the finest golfer in the world between the mid-1970s and mid-1980s, a period in which he won eight Majors and was elected US Player of the Year on six occasions.

Watson's accurate long game, upright swing, exceptional shot-making and confident putting were well suited to the US Tour schedule, where he won 34 events, but he particularly excelled at links golf. He had a slow start to his professional career but won his first Major – the 1975 British Open at Carnoustie – on his first attempt. His love affair with the tournament continued when he won again after an epic duel with Jack Nicklaus at Turnberry in 1977 before scooping the Masters in the same year. In 1980 he collected his third Open title at Muirfield and in the following year he won the Masters again, defeating Johnny Miller and Jack Nicklaus.

1982 was a particularly fruitful year for Watson, who picked up the claret jug again at Troon and won the US Open at Pebble Beach, birdying from the rough on the 17th and then again at the long 18th to snatch the title from the grasp of his arch-rival, Jack Nicklaus, who commented, 'You little son of a bitch. You're something else. I'm proud of you,' in spite of the fact that Watson had just denied Jack a record fifth Open title.

Watson won his last Major at Birkdale in 1983, his majestic long-iron shot on the final hole landing firmly on the green to allow him a one-shot victory over Andy Bean and Hale Irwin. He was in contention again at St Andrews 12 months later against Seve Ballesteros but was undone at the 17th when his second shot landed on the road, beside a wall, opening the way for Ballesteros to win the title. Also in 1984, he finished second in the Masters behind Ben Crenshaw and won three times on the US Tour.

Watson played in four Ryder Cups and in 1999 joined the US Seniors' Tour, where he continues his remarkable success, having won the Seniors' Tour and Senior PGA Championships.

— WOMEN DRIVERS —

During the 1975 Walker Cup at St Andrews, an elderly district nurse mistakenly drove her old jalopy onto the Old Course. Seeing the crowds, she panicked and attempted to escape, but she couldn't find her way out and drove straight into a pot bunker.

— AS IT LIES —

The most fundamental rule of golf is Rule 13.1, which states, 'The ball shall be played as it lies, except as otherwise provided in the Rules.' There are, however, a number of exceptions, as follows:

- In the winter months, or when rain or snow have badly affected the surface of the fairways, the course might introduce 'preferred lies'. This allows the golfer to lift the ball, clean it if necessary and replace it within 6in of where it landed but no nearer the hole. If there are no preferred lies, the golfer is not permitted to lift and clean, other than on the putting green, where this is allowed.

- Water hazards. Of these, there are two types: water hazard and lateral water hazard. The former is defined by yellow stakes and includes open water – ditch, pond, river etc – that is on or crosses the fairway. If a ball lands in this, clearly the golfer has the option of splashing out, but usually he will drop behind it (incurring a one-stroke penalty) in line with the point of entry. In a lateral water hazard, where it is impossible to drop a ball behind the hazard, the golfer can drop beside it, but no nearer the hole, and again incur a one-stroke penalty.

- If a ball is lost, the golfer is allowed five minutes to search for it. If unsuccessful, he must return to the spot from where he hit the shot and replay it, under a one-stroke penalty. If he fears that the ball might be lost when he hits it, he can play a 'provisional' ball, in case the original cannot be found, and incur a one-stroke penalty.

- In a bunker, the golfer is not permitted to smooth the sand behind the ball or to touch the sand with his club; he must instead play the shot as it lies.

- If the ball lands in the trees, the golfer may not break or bend any branches to improve his swing. He can, however, remove any 'loose impediments', such as twigs or leaves, as long as this does not result in the ball moving. If it does, he suffers a two-stroke penalty.

- If a ball is 'out of bounds' (ie beyond a boundary fence or ditch, usually marked by white posts), the player must return to the spot from where he hit the original shot and replay it, under a penalty of one stroke.

- A golfer can declare his ball 'unplayable' at any point, except when it is in a water hazard. He can then either drop the ball from shoulder height within two club lengths of where the ball lies (although not nearer the hole), drop the ball behind where it lies with no limit as to how far back he can go, or go back to where he hit the original shot and try again. Each option carries a one-stroke penalty.

One of the most famous examples of the 'as it lies' rule being enforced was in the 1949 British Open at Sandwich, where Irishman Harry Bradshaw shot 69 in the first round and started his second round with four straight fours. At the fifth hole, his ball landed in the bottom half of a broken beer bottle in the rough. Although he could have dropped the ball, as the broken bottle counted as a 'moveable obstruction', he decided he had to play the shot as it lay, smashing the glass in the process and propelling the ball barely twenty yards. He was so unnerved by this that he took a six and shot 77 for the day. His 68 and 70 in the final rounds took him to a playoff with Bobby Locke that Bradshaw lost. Had Bradshaw asked for an official ruling, he could have avoided the six and perhaps won his only British Open title.

— THE GOLF SWING —

The golf swing is, clearly, at the very heart of the game. Books are published on a regular basis – usually by the latest big name – to explain the mechanics and motion of the swing, and they often make it appear a simple affair. However, even today, after over 150 years of experimentation and adaptation, top golfers' swings can be remarkably dissimilar in execution and appearance. Compare, for instance, Colin Montgomerie's smooth, unruffled movement through the ball; John Daly's backswing, which almost touches the ground before he unleashes another 300-yarder; Nick Faldo's metronomic, consistently replicated swing; and Jim Furyk's action, which, as mentioned earlier, David Feherty once likened to 'an octopus falling out of a tree'. Yet all these players have succeeded at the highest level with their own means of getting the ball onto the green, as success depends more on the ability to repeat (ie 'groove') the swing than one's technical orthodoxy or elegance of playing.

In golf's earlier days, the swing was to a degree a function of the available technology. The first generally regarded style was the 'St Andrews Swing', inaugurated back in the days of the hard feathery ball, which had a leather cover and no

— THE GOLF SWING (CONT'D) —

dimples and with which it was very difficult to achieve loft. The favoured technique in those days was to hit the ball with a flat, roundabout swing in a sweeping motion, with the ball further back in the stance than today, and with a closed stance – ie with the left foot slightly in front of the right (all descriptions here refer to right-handed golfers). This not only kept the ball low (an advantage on the windy Scottish links) but also resulted in an accurate draw and maximum distance.

The arrival of the gutta-percha ball – the 'guttie' – in 1848 had a gradual impact on the nature of the swing. As well as being much cheaper to produce, it flew higher in the air and, as golfers began to realise, it flew further when it was slightly nicked. Players then began to cut patterns into their balls to achieve distance, but it wasn't until the emergence of the great Harry Vardon that the basic nature of the swing changed. Vardon possessed a much more upright swing than his contemporaries and, using an open stance, could hit the ball higher, further and straighter. He also employed the 'overlapping grip', where the little finger of his right hand overlapped the index finger of his left, giving him a grip that today remains by far the most common method of holding the club.

The next great champion, Bobby Jones, also had an upright, rhythmic swing but much more body rotation and wristiness than Vardon, partly in response to using the hickory-shafted clubs common at the time, which produced a lot of torque. By the time Byron Nelson was developing his game in the early 1930s, steel-shafted clubs had been declared legal and, given that they produced much less torque, Nelson's swing required less turning of the body, less hand action and more lower-body action. Thus was developed the modern swing.

Ben Hogan, who possessed an almost perfect swing and whose classic book *Five Lessons: The Modern Fundamentals Of Golf*, published in the late 1950s, is often cited as the classic golf instruction book, introduced the notion of the 'swing plane', which required a wider stance, weaker grip and a position that was less upright than that adopted in earlier stances. From this, he developed a low flight and slight fade, which, along with his obsession with practice, gave him a reliability and controllability unmatched, perhaps, until the coming of Tiger Woods.

Then Jack Nicklaus changed the standard swing again. He utilised a stronger grip than Hogan, with a higher plane and a wide swing arc, extending his left arm and cocking his wrists as late as possible on the backswing, while his follow-through resulted in a spine-threatening 'reverse C'. This was the swing adopted generally through most of the 1970s and 1980s, until relatively unknown coach David Ledbetter remodelled Nick Faldo's swing and substituted control for power. Faldo developed more of a compact, rotary action, using his legs for support rather than power and finishing up in a straight-on position rather than the 'reverse C'. His swing is economic and efficient, leaving very little to chance, and Ledbetter became a guru to many top professionals.

Of today's top golfers, perhaps the most stylish and effective swingers of the club, combining harmony and power, are Seve Ballesteros, Fred Couples, Ernie Els and, of course, Tiger Woods, who combines Nicklaus's power with Faldo's control.

— READ ALL ABOUT IT —

There are so many golf books in print, many of them of a very high standard, that it's difficult to know where to start in making a selection, but here's a taster of what's available. Bear in mind, however, that this is more than a John Daly tee-shot length away from being anything like comprehensive.

There are several different categories, the first being the ubiquitous how-to-play guide. These are usually (but not always) written by well-known golfers, employ glossy, action-packed colour photographs of the golfer in question, and impart the secret of the golf swing, bunker play, putting, long and short irons, uphill and downhill lies, and all the other aspects of the game that you'll need to know in order to whack a ball around a course. Some such volumes are blessedly simple, while others require a thesaurus and a scientific dictionary. Examples include Dave Pelz's *Putting Bible* and *Short Game Bible*, and Harvey Penick's *Little Red Golf Book*, an inspirational, anecdotal collection of lessons and teachings from the late golfing guru. Other good titles are Gary McCord's amusing *Golf For Dummies*, David Ledbetter's *The Golf Swing* (including tips and techniques from the world's leading coach), John Jacobs' *The Golf Swing Simplified* (featuring advice from the father of the European Tour and ex-Ryder Cup captain), Bob Rotella's *Golf Is Not A Game Of Perfect* (a study of the mental side of the game by the leading USPGA Tour psychologist), Ernie Els' *Complete Short Game* (in which the Big Easy gives tips on chipping, pitching, bunker play and putting), Tiger Woods' *How I Play Golf* (learn from the great man) and Greg Norman's *Advanced Golf* (play the game the White Shark way). Also, age shall not wither the classics, such as Ben Hogan and Herbert Warren Wind's massively influential *Five Lessons: The Modern Fundamentals Of Golf*, Tommy Armour's *How To Play Your Best Golf All The Time*, Jack Nicklaus's *Golf My Way* and Kathy Whitworth's *Golf For Women*.

Second, there are the golf reference books. For those interested in the various Tours, the Media Guides that these provide on an annual basis offer enough detailed information and statistics on the players and tournaments to make you go boss-eyed by page 20. The annual *World Of Professional Golf*, meanwhile, is another massive, information-packed tome that contains statistics, rankings and reports on all the players and major Tour matches for the preceding year, while the annual *Royal And Ancient Golfers' Handbook* is an invaluable reference, although its remit is wider than the world of professional golf. None of these are exactly bedtime reading. What will, however, keep you awake are books such as the beautifully produced, elegantly written and authoritative *The World Atlas Of Golf*, Derek Lawrenson's comprehensive *The Complete Encyclopedia Of Golf* and the Royal and Ancient's *Golf Rules Illustrated*, a successful attempt to demystify the rules of golf through drawings of hypothetical situations and the rulings thereon. The bookshelves groan with other works of reference on the various tournaments and competitions worldwide, as well as guides on where to play, with advice on courses – how to get to them, what they're like, and so on.

Then there are the biographies and autobiographies, some of which tend to the anodyne and self-serving but many of which reveal the motivations, passions and competitive rivalries of professional golf. Some of the more relatively recent in this genre are *Driven: The Definitive Biography Of Nick Faldo* by Dale Concannon; *Zinger* by Paul Azinger, relating his battle with cancer; *A Feel For The Game* by Ben Crenshaw; *Payne Stewart: The Authorised Biography* by Tracey Stewart and Ken Abraham; *The Chosen One: Tiger Woods And The Dilemma Of Greatness* by David Owen (no false modesty here); Kathlene Bissell's *Fred Couples* (the life of 'Boom Boom'); Lauren St John's *Shark: The Biography of Greg Norman*; and Colin Montgomerie's *The Real Monty*. If you want to understand caddies, look no further than John Feinstein's *Caddy For Life*, a biography of Tom Watson's caddy Bruce Edwards, who died in 2004. As for the legends of the game, highlights here are *The Bobby Jones Story* by OB Keeler, Byron Nelson's own *How I Played The Game* and James Dodson's *Ben Hogan: An American Life*. Later luminaries of golf Arnold Palmer and Jack Nicklaus have also penned autobiographies, the former writing *A Golfer's Life* and the latter the unsurprisingly titled *Jack Nicklaus*. Try Amazon if you can't get them at your local bookstore.

There are other books that aren't strictly (auto)biographical but concentrate on specific golfing episodes. One such is Mark James' *Inside The Bear Pit*, an account of his captaincy at the 1999 Brookline Ryder Cup, while Lawrence Donegan's entertaining *Four-Iron In My Soul* narrates the author's caddying duties for Ross Drummond on the 1996 European Tour. Other such books include the excellent and perceptive John Feinstein trilogy, comprising *A Good Walk Spoiled*, an account of the 1994 USPGA Tour that won the William Hill Sports Book of the Year Award in the UK; *The Majors*, which covers the four Majors in 1998; and *Open*, which tells the story of the first US Open to be played on a public course, Bethpage, in 2002. *Bud, Sweat And Tees*, by Alan Shipnuck, meanwhile, is an account of the fast-living Rich Beem's rookie year on the 1996 USPGA Tour and his unlikely triumph at the Kemper Open. US Tour golfer Esteban Toledo's rookie year on the USPGA Tour is well covered by Michael D'Antonio in *Tin Cup Dreams*. Now out of print but worth hunting down is the inimitable George Plimpton's *The Bogey Man*, covering his experiences in the 1960s on west coast pro-ams. David Gould's *Q School Confidential* penetrates the torture chamber that was the US Qualifying School

— READ ALL ABOUT IT (CONT'D) —

in 1998. And so the list continues, with other titles devoted to the Seniors' Tour (eg *Diamonds In The Rough* by Mark Shaw) and the LPGA Tour (eg Jim Burnett's *Tee Times*) as well as numerous other aspects of the game of golf.

Fiction is not quite so well covered (discounting the saintly PG Wodehouse, mentioned elsewhere in this book), but *Golf In The Kingdom* by Michael Murphy – about the mystical golfer and philosopher Shivas Irons – is well worth reading. So, too, are *The Legend Of Bagger Vance* by Steven Pressfield, centred on a fictional match between Walter Hagen, Bobby Jones and Rannolph Judah, whose philosopher caddy is the eponymous Vance; William Hallberg's *Perfect Lies*, an anthology of short stories on the game; and *Miracle On The 17th Green* by James Patterson and Peter Dejonge, on an amateur golfer who wins a place on the US Senior Tour at the cost of a shaky marriage. In this category, although not exactly fiction but beautifully written is the incomparable John Updike's *Golf Dreams*, which is a lyrical and affectionate collection of essays on golf in all its diversity by one of America's greatest living writers.

Then there are the whimsical, off-the-wall and trivia titles, a list of which would cover several pages and which it would be invidious to select here. Just visit your local bookstore or amazon.com to discover just how wonderful and varied are the imaginations and obsessions of all those authors who love the game of golf.

— FIVE FEARSOME BRITISH BUNKERS —

The most notorious British bunker is probably the 17th at St Andrews, and all links courses have several pot bunkers designed to snare the unwary. Here are five particularly nasty examples of the genre:

- **Third hole at Prestwick, Ayrshire (482 yards, par five).** Having safely negotiated the first hole alongside the Ayr–Glasgow railway line of this famous old course, the golfer is then faced with the third, containing the huge Cardinal bunker, which, shored up with wood, stretches the entire length of the fairway at the dogleg point.

- **Sixth hole at Addington, Surrey (342 yards, par four).** A sleepy parkland course near London, with a bunker so deep on the sixth hole that PG Wodehouse once wrote a letter addressed from 'c/o bunker at the 6th, Addington'.

- **Fourth hole at Royal North Devon, Westward Ho! (349 yards, par four).** The oldest golf course in England contains, on the fourth hole, the Cape bunker, which is sleepered and extends 60 yards across the fairway.

- **Fourth hole, Royal St George's, Kent (497 yards, par five).** This British Open course has, on the fourth hole, an enormous bunker reputed to be the deepest in Britain. It is 20ft high and has wooden slats at its face.

- **16th hole, Chart Hills, Surrey (506 yards, par five).** Designed by Nick Faldo, the 16th hole on this championship course contains no fewer than 19 bunkers.

(My personal *bête noire* is a short hole at Ayr Belleisle, which, once I had clambered down a ladder into the pot bunker at the front of the green, extracted nine shots from me before I could escape. I remember it with horror, as I am sure do the ladies waiting behind on the tee who had to listen to my language.)

— BILLY BLOWS IT —

Three-time Majors winner Billy Casper had a few problems in the first round of the 2005 Masters. Winner of the tournament in 1970, Casper set several records on his way around the course at Augusta. Not only did he take 106 strokes to complete his round – at 34 over par, the highest score in Masters history – but he also shot the worst nine-hole score (57) and the highest score at a single hole (14 at the par-three 16th). He also set the record for the biggest difference between a player's best and worst scores in the tournament (40 shots).

The 73-year-old, who, with 51 victories, is sixth on the all-time PGA Tour list, was philosophical about his disastrous trudge around Augusta. He declined to sign his card and was disqualified. 'I'm taking it with me and I'm framing it,' he promised. 'I'm going to put it in my scrapbook.'

— HOWARD HUGHES, GOLFER —

Howard Hughes – inventor, aircraft designer, film producer, famed seducer of beautiful women, billionaire and, ultimately, weird recluse – had one over-riding passion in life: golf. The gangly, profoundly driven youth was given his first golf club by his dad – inventor of a hugely lucrative granite-busting drill – at the age of nine. By the time he was 19 years old, his parents had both died, he had inherited millions and he spent most of his time at Houston Country Club, playing and practising the game.

Although an average putter, he could hit the ball up to 300 yards and played off a handicap of two. The young man was obsessed with the game, to the extent that he designed his own clubs and cut open golf balls to analyse their make-up, attempting to improve the core by substituting cork.

Hughes moved to LA in 1926 with his first wife, Ella Rice, and bought a Spanish villa next to the fairway of the Wilshire Country Club. When his film *Hell's Angels* – featuring a dramatic scene that involved simulated dogfights over Los Angeles and that provoked huge excitement for the spectators on the ground – was being shot in 1928, Hughes was too busy perfecting his swing at a driving range to bother watching. His first marriage ended in 1929, Ella suffering the existence of a golf widow as well as being a victim of Hughes' serial philandering. Indeed, he was deadly serious about his golf, positioning film crews on overhead blimps to record his practice sessions on the golf course, and he hired Ralph Guldhal, winner of the 1937 and 1938 US Opens and 1939 Masters, as his personal coach.

In 1931 Hughes filed a multi-million-dollar lawsuit against film director Howard Hawks, claiming that Hawks' film *The Dawn Patrol* had been plagiarised from *Hell's Angels*. As Hawks was preparing to tee off at Lakeside GC, he received a message saying that Hughes would like to join him on the course. 'Tell him I don't want to play with him,' said a justifiably angry Hawks. 'If you play, he'll call the suit off,' responded one of Hughes' aides. The two Hollywood titans teed off together, and the result of their discussions during the round was the movie *Scarface*.

Hughes also developed an unlikely friendship with Gene Sarazen. The laconic, 6ft 3in Texan towered over the squat, voluble squire, but they nevertheless hit it off, Hughes offering the master golfer of the era flying lessons in exchange for golfing hints and tips. Indeed, Hughes' explanation of the aerodynamics of aeroplane lift-off is reputed to have inspired Sarazen to conceive the idea behind the sand wedge, a club that revolutionised the game in the 1930s and changed the shape of golf courses across the world.

One of Hughes' many lovers was Katherine Hepburn, herself a more than capable golfer who regularly shot in the low 70s. In his dogged pursuit of the film star, Hughes once landed his two-seater, single-prop Sikorsky plane on the eighth fairway of the exclusive Bel-Air Country Club and asked Hepburn, playing with her coach, 'Can I join as a third?' Three months later, Hepburn had moved into Hughes' Wilshire villa.

Ever an obsessive, Hughes abruptly gave up playing golf in 1939. A near-fatal aeroplane crash in 1946 – when his out-of-control, self-piloted XF 11 narrowly avoided LA Country Club and demolished a section of Beverley Hills – persuaded him to throw away his clubs. His burns and injuries led to his subsequent codeine addiction and withdrawal from the world.

Hughes' interest in the game continued, however, and in 1967, as a hermit occupying the top floors of the Desert Inn in Las Vegas, he bought the hotel and its 'Tournament of Champions' golf event. He was incensed when Arnold Palmer and Jack Nicklaus moved with the tournament the following year to Rancho La Costa, stating, 'It is my desire to establish Las Vegas as the golf capital of the world.' This, of course, did not happen.

Two years before Hughes died, in 1976, his office was burgled. The perpetrators did not discover the riches that they'd hoped for, discovering instead largely worthless memorabilia including obscure golf trophies that Hughes had retained, considering them worth more than any of the billions he had accrued during his bizarre and brilliant lifetime.

— ROUND IN 18 —

'You drive for show and putt for dough,' as the old maxim has it. Well, the guys below must have cleaned up, as they're the only players to have played official USPGA Tour events and gone around 18 holes while taking only 18 putts apiece:

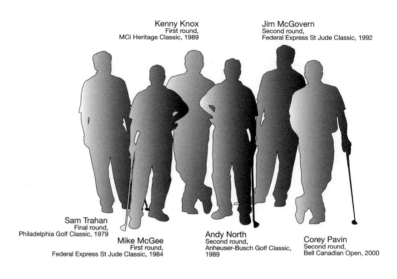

Kenny Knox
First round,
MCI Heritage Classic, 1989

Jim McGovern
Second round,
Federal Express St Jude Classic, 1992

Sam Trahan
Final round,
Philadelphia Golf Classic, 1979

Mike McGee
First round,
Federal Express St Jude Classic, 1984

Andy North
Second round,
Anheuser-Busch Golf Classic,
1989

Corey Pavin
Second round,
Bell Canadian Open, 2000

On the same tour, the fewest putts taken over nine holes are seven. The two record-holders for this feat are:

- **Bill Nary** – back nine, third round, El Paso Open, 1952
- **Stan Utley** – front nine, second round, Air Canada Championship, 2002

— SCORES FROM HELL —

All average golfers know that a low-scoring streak is almost always followed by a disaster, as if the god of golf becomes irritated by the player's unwarranted swelling of self-confidence and has to give a reminder of one's fallibility and meaninglessness in the golfing scheme of things. 'Oh well, I knew it was too good to be true' is the normal response as another ball plops into the nearest pond. Be reassured, however, that top golfers are also sufferers from this iron law, as the following examples demonstrate.

At the 1927 Shawnee Open, Tommy Armour, an obdurate and often pig-headed player, decided that his best shot on a particular hole was to aim down the right-hand side of the fairway and draw the ball back towards the green. Having hit his first five tee shots out of bounds on the right, he continued with his belief in this judgment. When the next five tee shots did exactly the same thing, he came to the conclusion that his decision was perhaps not the correct one and aimed his 11th straight onto the fairway. He collected a score of 22 for the hole.

Arnold Palmer reached the ninth tee of the 1961 Los Angeles Open in his second round and was looking for a birdie on the 418-yard, par-four hole. Instead of playing sensibly and opting for an iron, however, he selected a three-wood. His first shot went out of bounds on the right and his second was also OB, this time on the left. Still clutching the three-wood, he hit his next two tee shots and the same pattern occurred. For his fifth tee shot, he finally reached for an iron and connected with the fairway. He ended up with a 12. A commemorative plaque marks the spot, although presumably Palmer didn't visit it too often.

At the 1982 Heritage Classic, Ben Crenshaw was on the 14th tee on his last round. The hole – a 165-yard par three – was, in the windy conditions, a decent three-iron, but Ben opted for a four-iron. His first tee shot ended up in the water at the front of the green, as did his next three. Reasoning that he might have underclubbed, he hit his fifth shot with a three-iron and bounced over the green. He eventually bagged 11 for the hole, then went on to take an eight at the 15th, somewhat unnerved by the experience.

In the 1982 Martini International on the European Tour, when Greg Norman was on the 17th tee he reached the top of his backswing and, disturbed by the click of a camera, sent the ball into long, ferny grass. His next shot hit a tree and dropped into an unplayable lie. He dropped into an even more unplayable position. His third shot found more

— SCORES FROM HELL (CONT'D) —

undergrowth, as did his fourth, requiring another penalty drop. His fifth connected well with the ball but hit a tree and there it was, back in the sticky stuff. Deciding not to be macho any longer, he pitched out sideways onto the fairway, chipped on and took two putts. The cost of this visit to the jungle? 14 strokes.

At the 1998 Bay Hill Invitational, the inimitable John Daly provided the highlight of the tournament as he attempted to cut the corner of a large lake on Bay Hill's 543-yard, par-five sixth hole and instead, in true *Tin Cup* fashion, plopped six shots into the water. He took a remarkable 18 strokes to finish the hole.

Tom Weiskopf, winner of the 1973 British Open at Troon, was on the 12th tee at Augusta in the first round of the US Masters. The hole, part of the Amen Corner trilogy, is a par-three, 155-yard shot to a narrow green behind a wide creek. Weiskopf's tee shot, of course, ended in the water, whereupon he moved to the ball-dropping zone and the ball again went into the water – as did the next three. Rather dispirited by this point, he finally got the ball on the green and signed for a 13.

The 13th hole at the 1978 US Masters proved unlucky for Tommy Nakajima. After hitting his ball into Rae's Creek, he was given five penalty shots on the hole for various infractions, including grounding a club and allowing the ball to hit his foot. As he staggered away to the 14th tee, he had taken 13 shots to complete the par-five hole. In 1984, he would take nine at the 17th at St Andrews, the bunker there forever after being known as 'the Sands of Nakajima'.

Finally, at the US Open at Cherry Hills in 1938, Ray Ainsley's approach shot to the 16th hole splashed into a fast-flowing stream. After several attempts to coax it out, he connected and sent the ball flying into a clump of bushes. His score of 19 is the highest score ever recorded for a single hole in the history of the US Open.

— ALLISS' HALL OF FAME: WALTER HAGEN —

Something of a playboy and *bon viveur*, Walter Hagen was also a fierce, nerveless competitor on the golf course. His deadly short game and accurate recovery shots unnerved opponents, and his easygoing manner masked a deep determination to win.

Hagen won his first Major at the 1914 US Open and won the title again in 1919. In that year he became the first-ever full-time American tournament professional, and the 1920s saw him at his peak. Although he never won another US Open, unable to overcome the obstacle of rival Bobby Jones, he won the USPGA a remarkable five times between 1921 and 1927 (Jones, an amateur, wasn't eligible for the tournament). That competition was then in the matchplay format, which was ideally suited to Hagen's self-confidence and ability to play his way seamlessly out of trouble.

During the 1920s, Hagen also won four Open titles in 1922, 1924, 1928 and 1929, becoming the first American to win the US and UK Opens in 1922. He was also captain of the inaugural US Ryder Cup team's victory over Britain in 1927 and played in all their matches until 1937.

With his chauffeur-driven Pierce–Arrow limousine, his flamboyant dress sense and his love of wine and women, Hagen created the modern notion of the sportsman as superstar. However, he lacked the self-importance and hint of petulance characteristic of many modern sportsmen. 'I never wanted to be a millionaire,' he once remarked; 'I just wanted to live like one.' Bobby Jones once admitted, 'I love to play with Walter. He goes along, chin up, smiling away, never grousing about his luck, playing the ball as he finds it.' Indeed, one of Hagen's pet phrases was 'Never hurry, never worry.' He died in Michigan at the age of 76. Gene Sarazen commented on his influence, 'It was Walter who made professional golf what it is.'

— TURNING JAPANESE —

At the 1983 Hawaii Open, Jack Renner was checking his card after completing his final round and was pretty sure that he'd won the tournament. The only person who could theoretically catch him was Isao 'the Tower' Aoki, who had just hit his second shot on the 18th, which landed 90 yards away from the pin. Aoki took out his pitching wedge and launched a perfect shot that rolled into the cup for an eagle and was enough to beat Renner by one shot and win the event. He became the first-ever Japanese golfer to win on the US Tour.

— IMPOSTORS —

Describing himself as a 'professional golfer' on his application form, Walter Danecki from Milwaukee turned up at qualifying for the 1965 British Open at Hillside Golf Club. He went around the course in 108 and, although the R&A smelled a rat and nominated a substitute for the second round, Walter was back on the first tee the next day and the R&A could do nothing about it. He began 7–7–8 and ran up a score of 113, failing to qualify for the Open by 75 strokes. 'I'm glad I played your small ball,' said Walter. 'If I'd played the big ball I'd have been all over the place.'

Eleven years later, at Formby, in a qualifying round for the 1976 British Open at Royal Birkdale, 46-year-old local crane driver Maurice Flitcroft – who had taken up the game 18 months earlier and had played all his golf on a local beach and scrubland – turned up also under the guise of a 'professional golfer'. Never having played 18 holes before in his life, he began the first two holes 11 and 12, on his way to carding 121. He then withdrew, stating, 'I have no chance of qualifying.' Somewhat ominously, echoing Schwarzenegger in *Terminator*, he added, 'I'll be back'. A reporter spoke to his mum that evening: 'I'm phoning about Maurice and the Open.' 'Oh yes,' said Mum. 'Has he won?'

In the 1983 qualifier for the British Open, a gentleman going under the name Gerald Hoppy and claiming to be from Switzerland teed off and completed the first nine holes in 63. Yes, under the wig, false moustache and heavy disguise was the indefatigable Maurice Flitcroft. You have to admire his persistence, but there have been no further sightings since then.

— GOLFING GRIPS —

1. Normal grip

2. Interlocking grip

3. Overlapping grip

— TOO EARLY...AND TOO LATE —

In the 1940 US Open, held at Canterbury Golf Club in Cleveland, Ohio, thunderclouds were building up on the horizon and a storm appeared likely. Two groups of three players – Johnny Bulle, Porky Oliver and Dutch Harrison; and Ky Laffoon, Duke Gibson and Claude Harmon – decided to start their final two rounds (both then played on the same day) 28 minutes early. They were all disqualified. Oliver shot 71 and would have made the playoff.

Seve Ballesteros had the opposite problem. The reigning British Open and Masters champion was due to tee off at Baltusrol, New Jersey, on the second day of the 1980 US Open. Apparently unaware of his tee-off time and stuck in heavy traffic on his way to the course, he sauntered onto the first tee only to find himself disqualified from the tournament for being seven minutes late.

— ST ANDREWS CADDIES —

The caddies at St Andrews in the late 19th century were a tough, hard-bitten lot. Fond of the odd dram, and often churlish on the course, they were a collection of endearing oddballs. The first recorded mention of caddies on the Old Course was in 1771, while the winner of the first Caddies Competition was Old Tom Morris in 1842. The motley cast of worthies included the following:

- **Willie 'Trap Door' Johnson,** who perfected a special boot with a hollow sole. He would declare a ball lost, scoop it up in his shoe trap and sell on the balls. His sole could conceal up to six golf balls.

- **'Poot' Chisolm,** whose guiding principle was 'With good porridge and a wee nip you're all right for life.' And so say all of us.

- **'Skippa' Stewart Fenton,** who, like many other caddies of his time, alternated his duties on the golf course with being a fisherman.

- **Alex 'Pint Size' Brown,** a man of small frame.

- **Willie Robertson,** known as 'Lang Willie' on account of his 6ft 2in size. He was never seen without his 'lum'- (chimney-) shaped hat.

- **David Anderson,** 'Auld Daw', father of three-time British Open winner Jamie and who, on his retirement, opened a ginger-beer stall (with something stronger on the side) on the ninth hole.

- **John 'Sodger' Smith McIntyre,** who used to caddy for Prime Minister AJ Balfour.

- **Archie 'Stumpie Eye' Stump,** who was half blind, and so not much help on the distances, but who had a strong pair of shoulders.

- **'Hole in 'is pocket',** who would drop a ball down his trouser leg and exclaim, in mock surprise, 'Here it is, sir.'

There were of course many others, such as 'Boozie' Chas and 'Wiggie' Ayton (no need to explain the origin of their nicknames), who contributed to the anarchic, uncouth but special atmosphere of the Old Course over a century ago.

For more information on St Andrews' caddies, read Richard MacKenzie's *A Wee Nip At The 19th Hole*. Fascinating stuff.

— PUTTING THE BOOT IN —

Two of the many parts of your body that you have to be aware of on the golf course are your feet, and what they're up to. These next two guys weren't.

During the 1921 British Open at St Andrews, English amateur Roger Wethered was backing away from the hole on the green when he stood on his ball. He was deducted one penalty stroke, tied for the title and lost the playoff to Jock Hutchinson.

Byron Nelson was playing in the 1946 US Open at Canterbury Golf Club, Ohio, when his caddie accidentally kicked the ball on the 16th hole, conceding a penalty stroke. Nelson was forced into a playoff against Lloyd Mangrum. Mangrum, of course, won.

— THE EASIEST SHOT? —
THE FOURTH PUTT

The most famous missed short putt in golf history was Doug Sanders' miss on the 18th at St Andrews in the 1970 British Open that allowed Jack Nicklaus to draw and beat him on a playoff. However, when the pressure is on, anyone is capable of whiffing from a short distance. Here are a few examples.

- In the 1889 British Open at Musselburgh, in the final round between Willie Park and Andrew Kirkaldy, Kirkaldy left his ball 1in from the hole. Without looking, he attempted to stroke it in with one hand, missed and dropped a shot. Had he putted, he would have won. As it was, he went into a playoff and lost to Park.

- In the 1913 US Open, Harry Vardon's missed putt from 3in contributed to a three-way tie and a win for Francis Ouimet, the US's first victory in the competition.

- In the final hole of the 1978 Masters, Hubert Green was faced with a three-foot putt to tie with Gary Player and force a playoff. As he lined up the putt, he was disturbed by a radio commentator. He turned away, refocused and missed.

- English touring pro Brian Barnes was on the eighth green of St Cloud during the 1968 French Open with a three-foot putt for par. Some demon must have entered the Englishman's brain, however, because a couple of minutes later he sunk the putt after 11 attempts. For a further ignominy, he was awarded a two-stroke penalty for standing astride the line of his putt.

— FIVE TOP GOLFING MOVIES —

Tin Cup (Ron Shelton, 1996)
Washed-up golf pro Roy 'Tin Cup' McAvoy (Kevin Costner) falls for shrink Molly (Rene Russo), who visits his dilapidated driving range in Texas for lessons. Unfortunately she is the girlfriend of Roy's arch-rival, smug and successful USPGA Tour golfer David Simms (Don Johnson). Roy regains his self-belief and his career is reignited, helped by Molly and his buddy Romeo Pesar (Cheech Marin). After several hilarious and moving cameos, Roy qualifies for the US Open and the movie concludes with a shoot-out between him and Simms

on the final round of the tournament. An unlikely tale but heartwarming and fun.

CADDYSHACK (HAROLD RAMIS, 1980)
A wildly anarchic comedy in which a vulgar land developer (Rodney Dangerfield) wants to build condominiums on the site of a wealthy golf club owned by the obnoxious Judge Smails (Ted Knight). Meanwhile, the greenkeeper (Bill Murray) is obsessed about destroying a dancing gopher (the real star of the movie). Caddy Danny (Michael O'Keefe) is trying to raise money to go to college, helped by pro Ty 'become the ball' Webb (Chevy Chase). The madcap, hilarious antics begin here. A cult classic.

THE LEGEND OF BAGGER VANCE (ROBERT REDFORD, 2000)
Set in the 1930s and revolving around ex-golf star and war veteran Ranulph Junuh (Matt Damon), who has fallen into drinking and gambling. His girlfriend Adele (Charlize Theron), whose wealthy father has committed suicide due to the Great Depression, is saddled with debts. To raise money, she decides to hold a golf exhibition match between Walter Hagen (Bruce McGill) and Bobby Jones (Joel Gresch), and Junuh is also invited to play, representing Savannah and assisted by poor, young, black caddie, and ultimately guru and guardian angel, Bagger Vance (Will Smith). Beautifully photographed, this is an inspiring, dreamlike movie about golf and redemption.

FOLLOW THE SUN (SIDNEY LANFIELD, 1951)
A biopic of Ben Hogan and his comeback to the pinnacle of US golf after a devastating car accident. It charts his life from a poor kid and caddy in Texas to his joining the professional Tour. Glenn Ford well conveys Hogan's aloofness and intensity and Anne Baxter is the perfect foil as his wife. Hogan himself hits the golf shots in the film. A motivational movie that generally avoids mawkishness.

DEAD SOLID PERFECT (BOBBY ROTH, 1988)
Based on Dan Jenkins' 1974 novel of the same name, this movie follows an unfocused, low-ranking, wild-partying US Tour golfer whose marriage is on the rocks. An insight into life on the Tour with a shrewd blend of humour and drama.

— THE DEATH OF A LEGEND —

Immediately recognisable on the golf course in his plus fours and tam o'shanter, Payne Stewart was an exuberant and flamboyant personality, a committed Christian and family man, and an exceptionally talented golfer, with 11 Tour victories, including three Majors, to his credit. He won his last Major – the US Open – in 1999, holing a putt on the final hole at Pinehurst to defeat Phil Mickelson by one stroke.

On the morning off 25 October 1999, when his co-owned Lear jet took off from Orlando to take him to the prestigious, season-ending Tour championship in Houston, it seemed a day like any other in the career of this multi-millionaire sportsman. Less than an hour later, however, the US Air Force at Eglin Air Force Base received a call from air traffic control informing them that the jet was travelling erratically and that there were no radio transmissions coming from the plane. An F16 was scrambled and, when it drew alongside no more than 100ft away from the plane, the pilot reported what appeared to be condensation or frost on the windows. All the evidence indicated that the plane had lost cabin pressure and that the two pilots and four occupants had fallen unconscious or had died from lack of oxygen.

The Air Force tracked the plane – which was clearly on autopilot and fluctuating in altitude – for more than two hours, until, having run out of fuel, the Lear jet spun out of the skies to crash at 600mph nose first into a field in South Dakota.

This was the fist significant air crash involving a US Tour golfer since the death of 'Champagne' Tony Lema after he won the 1964 British Open, and the professionals on the US Tour were shocked by the tragedy. At the Tour Championship, a lone bagpiper played a lament before the tournament and a special service was held to commemorate Stewart's life.

— GLOSSARY —

The lexicon of golf can appear incomprehensible to the uninitiated. Here is a selection of some of the terms used in the game (apart from swear words, which, although probably most common, have been excluded).

Ace – A hole in one.

Address – The position adopted before playing a shot.

Air shot – A swing that completely misses the ball but counts on the scorecard.

Albatross – Three under par on a hole, known as a 'double eagle' in the USA.

Apron – The area just in front of the green.

Back door – When a ball is holed by going around the lip of the cup and dropping in from the back end.

Back nine – The homeward (inward) nine holes on a golf course.

Baffy – Another name for a four-wood.

Bandit – A player who overstates his or her handicap to seek unfair advantage.

Better ball – In a fourball competition, the best score of two players.

Birdie – One under par on a hole.

Bogey – One over par on a hole.

Borrow – The degree to which a putt will have to deviate from a straight line due to the slope of the green.

Brassie – Another name for a two-wood.

Bunker – A hazard filled with sand.

Caddie – Someone hired to carry a golf bag and dispense advice, if required.

Carry – The distance from where the ball is struck to where it first lands.

Casual water – Standing water which is not a hazard or part of a hazard.

Chilli-dip – To fluff a lofted shot by hitting behind the ball.

Chip – A low-hit shot from around the green towards the pin.

Choke – To snatch defeat from the jaws of victory (ie to lose a match from a winning position).

Choke down – To grip lower on the club for greater control.

Cut – A point in a competition, usually at the halfway point, when the field is divided into those who remain and those who leave.

Divot – The clump of turf removed by a club when a shot is played.

Dogleg – A hole that changes direction, to the right or left, during its course.

Dormie – In matchplay, as many holes up as there are holes remaining.

Downhill lie – When the ball rests on a hill that goes down towards the target.

Draw – A deliberately flighted shot that curves to the left (for a right-handed golfer).

Eagle – Two under par on a hole.

Explosion shot – A shot made from a lie that's buried in a bunker where the club digs and displaces a large amount of sand.

Fade – A deliberately flighted shot that curves to the right (for a right-handed golfer).

Fairway – The area of cut grass between the tee and the green.

Follow-through – The forward motion of the swing after impact with the ball.

Fore! – A shouted warning to other golfers that your shot is heading towards them. Often the direction is included, ie 'Fore right!' The word is a contraction of the 16th-century term 'Beware before', uttered in order to alert soldiers to cannonballs flying over their heads in the enemy's direction.

Fried egg – A lie in a sand bunker where the landing of the ball has splashed the immediate sand away, leaving the ball resting in the middle of a crater.

Front nine – The opening (outward) nine holes on a golf course.

Gimme – An easy putt conceded in matchplay.

Green – An area of grass prepared as a putting area.

Gross – The total score before the handicap is deducted.

Guttie – A type of golf ball made of gutta percha that made the old 'featheries' obsolete.

Hacker – A poor golfer.

Handicap – A system whereby players of differing abilities can play each other on level terms. The better a player, the lower his handicap and vice versa.

Honour – The player who plays first from the tee, usually the winner of the previous hole.

Hook – A mishit that which curves sharply to the left (for a right-handed player).

Interlocking grip – A grip whereby the player holds the club with the little finger of the left hand interlocked with the forefinger of the right hand (for right-handed golfers).

Jigger – Another name for a four-iron.

Lag – To play a putt deliberately near but short of the hole.

Lateral water hazard – A water hazard that runs parallel to the fairway.

Lie – Where the ball stops after a stroke. 'Play it as it lies' is the basic principle of golf.

Links – Strictly defined as seaside golf courses situated between the sea and 'cultivable land'.

Local rules – Particular rules that apply to particular courses.

Loft – The angle of a club face.

Long iron – Irons numbered one to four.

Loose impediments – Natural objects on the course, such as stones, that aren't fixed in place.

Matchplay – A style of play where the game is decided by the number of holes won and lost.

Medal – A strokeplay competition, mainly held on a monthly basis at golf clubs.

Mid-iron – Irons numbered five to seven.

Mulligan – A second chance off the first tee, to be taken on with the agreement of all players.

Niblick – Another term for a nine-iron.

Out of bounds – Describes anywhere outside what is defined as the area of the course, usually marked by white posts.

Par – The standard score for each hole and the course.

Pin-high – Describes a shot that travels the distance between the player and the pin.

Pitch-lifted – Describes a high shot from the green to the pin.

Pitch mark – A mark left by a ball when it lands on the green.

Pot bunker – A deep bunker with steep sides, usually found on links courses.

Preferred lies – Regulation concerning the ability to lift a ball, normally in wet conditions or during winter.

Provisional ball – If a ball is feared lost or out of bounds, a second, provisional ball may be played.

Pull – A mishit shot that travels in a straight line to the right (for a right-handed player).

Push – A mishit shot that travels in a straight line to the left (for a right-handed player).

R&A – Abbreviation of the Royal and Ancient Golf Club of St Andrews, the governing body of the game outside USA and Mexico.

Rabbit – A novice or poor golfer.

Rough – Unmown grass outside the fairway. **Fairway rough** is the level in between the rough and the fairway.

Rub of the green – An unexpected bounce of the ball after it hits the ground.

Scratch – Describes a player with a handicap of zero.

Shank – Mishit shot where the ball comes off the junction of the hosel and the clubface and usually veers off at right-angles to the target.

Short iron – irons numbered eight and nine and all wedges.

Slice – A mishit shot that curves sharply to the right (for a right-handed player).

Stroke index – The difficulty rating of all holes on a course, from 1 to 18.

Strokeplay – A style of play where the game is decided by the number of strokes played.

Sweet spot – The area of the club face with the perfect hitting spot.

Tee – The (usually raised) area from where the first shot on each hole is played.

Topped – Describes a mishit shot that travels along the ground.

Trap – US term for a *bunker*.

Uphill lie – Where the ball comes to rest on a slope above the target.

USGA – Abbreviation of the United States Golf Association, responsible for the rules of golf in the USA and Mexico.

Yips – A nervous state that prevents a player from putting normally. Bernhard Langer is probably the best-known sufferer of the condition.

— INDEX —